Painting
With
Purpose

PRENTICE-HALL INTERNATIONAL, INC., *London*
PRENTICE-HALL OF AUSTRALIA, PTY., LTD., *Sydney*
PRENTICE-HALL OF CANADA, LTD., *Toronto*
PRENTICE-HALL FRANCE, S.A.R.L., *Paris*
PRENTICE-HALL OF JAPAN, INC., *Tokyo*
PRENTICE-HALL DE MEXICO, S.A., *Mexico City*

Painting
With
Purpose

MORRIS DAVIDSON

Prentice-Hall, Inc.

Englewood Cliffs, New Jersey

FRONTISPIECE: Morris Davidson, *Painting of Linear Pattern*

Preface

This volume is intended as an exercise book for painters and students with some background and experience. It is not addressed to beginners. Its point of view is contemporary but it is also linked, by some of the principles advocated, to the art of other times and cultures. It is based upon a long experience in formulating for students effective drills involving various esthetic and plastic problems. It is not pretended that the exercises will in themselves insure the production of works of art, but they will, if used intelligently, develop in the student (as they have in hundreds who have experienced them in my classes) some sense of rhythmic and spatial order and avoidance of commonplace picture-making.

For more than a decade the words "contemporary" and "modern" have been associated in the popular mind with two or three styles of non-figurative painting which may be grouped together as "Abstract Expressionism." This school of painting places heavy emphasis upon individual feeling and unconscious expression without restraint, the thought behind this being that conscious, controlled art is sterile and demodé. The cumulative result of such esthetic philosophy has been the prolific production of canvases so resembling each other as to be anonymous. In the effort to run away from conscious, thoughtful painting, the daring innovators have all taken refuge in the same kinds of "innovation."

The objective here is to unearth certain principles of painting which give esthetic meaning to the art. Such principles are like the elements of music where the terms rhythm, interval, counterpoint, etc., have specific meanings. In painting there are principles of space-relation, tension, rhythm, balance, and interval (among others), all of which should be part of the training of the painter. The intention, then, is to restate these principles by adapting them to contemporary idioms. The means of achieving this lie in the exercises designed to make the painter explore each principle as a sort of grammatical background for his own expression.

It was considered most practicable to organize the material into several sections. The first five chapters form a unit dealing with elements of representational painting from a contemporary viewpoint, and including painting exercises designed to afford experience with these elements. Part II is an exposition of some principles of contemporary non-figurative painting. The exercises here are restricted to charcoal preparations for the major working-section of the book. This is the chapter entitled *Twelve Painting Projects*. Many years of observation of the efficiency of these projects in developing painters justifies the belief that they constitute a practical course in painting composition. But their significance is lost without the exposition of the chapters preceding.

The exercises are given in outline form, without too much specific or detailed direction, and often without reproductions or prototypes. This is not an oversight, but is deliberate; the purpose is to avoid setting academic patterns for students to imitate. Greater latitude and resourcefulness will be encouraged by clear statement of objectives rather than by model demonstrations. But where the framework for the exercise may be difficult to grasp from verbal description, diagrams are shown in the text. Moreover, in the chapter on color the meaning of the text could not be made clear without color reproduction.

The illustrations, in addition to the author's own, were chosen to clarify the objectives of the exercises; they are not to be considered as an anthology of the world's great art. Many are acknowledged masterpieces, some are lesser works by celebrated artists, still others are works by little known artists. The latter have been selected for their instructional value, their clear exposition of the artists' principles and objectives.

The author wishes to express his indebtedness to the many museums and private collections that have provided him with reproductions. He would also like to record his gratitude to his wife Anne who, besides her useful criticism, has assisted him in every detail of the manuscript's preparation.

M. D.

Contents

Photographs
of Paintings

Painting
With
Purpose

Part *I*

Figure 1

Piet Mondrian, *Painting*

Division
of Surface Area

1   The design of rectangular spaces is the
hallmark of our culture since the First World War. We
accept without question the arrangement of interiors, the
blocks of office buildings, and the inventive rectangular
patterns of modern store fronts and break-fronts alike. The
grill-work and rears of our automobiles and the dust
jackets of books reflect the same dedication to rectangular
relationships of size and proportion. But while everybody,
whether in Paris or Salina, Kansas, recognizes this somewhat
mechanical esthetic as the sophisticated look of our
century, not everybody is aware that it stems from the work
of a Belgian painter (and perhaps one or two Russian
artists) who sought to express, not design, but the restraint
and harmony of pure painting—painting rid of subject
matter, of virtuosity, even of dramatic impact. The Belgian
painter was, of course, Mondrian.

Let us look at a typical composition of Mondrian
(Fig. 1) and take a moment to review his ideas and intentions.
The putting together of rectangles of varied size appears to

be based upon a geometrical order deriving from Greek architecture. It is therefore termed Classical. According to Mondrian, primary colors, red, yellow, and blue, represent structure; white, black, and gray, the surrounding space. Proportion, variation, and position are of the essence. Only the horizontal and vertical are employed in the search for purity of expression. It is often said of Mondrian's designs that they are mathematical equations in paint. He himself renounced the intellect in creative expression and declared that only sensibility and spirit could produce true art. He sought to express the absolute, the divine. His colleague, Van Doesburg said, when announcing their new art, that there was a need for painting composed only of horizontal and vertical lines, "that is to say, a work composed of two universal directions which, by their variations and by the manner in which they are organized—such organization is obviously not determined by hand or brain, but by the emotions—express the divine in the shortest time and in the most direct fashion." [1]

However novel Mondrian's art appeared to the public a generation ago —to students of painting its form was the logical end (perhaps the *reductio ad absurdum*) of centuries-old efforts to resolve one basic tenet of pictorial composition—the division of the surface area. This element of design is not restricted to a single era or a single cultural tradition. It is basic; without the capacity to combine dissimilar quantities in a balanced unity the painter's recourse is apt to be either dramatic self-expression or clever performance. But the artist who thinks of himself as a constructor—a maker of form—whatever his cultural milieu unconsciously allies himself to a tradition of picture making that is without boundaries in time and place. A few examples from various cultures will show different modes of expressing this universal esthetic principle.

First is a Persian miniature attributed to Bihzad, a scene of mourning (Fig. 2). While not as "pure" as Mondrian's painting it is at least as inventive in its organization of the surface—and incidentally antedates his by five centuries. Here the rectangular division of the surface is enhanced by the several diagonals to provide greater variety of shape. The figures are disposed in such manner that their silhouettes are made to create sharply defined patterns of negative space—spaces around and between forms. Even the legend in the upper right corner occupies a rectangle which imaginatively alters the space below. The severity of the composition is offset by

---

[1] Quoted in *L'Art Abstrait* by Marcel Brion (Edition Albin Michel, 1956), p. 92. (Trans. by author)

Figure 2

Persian Miniature, *Khamsa of Nizami*. Reproduced by permission of the Trustees of the British Museum

the rounded forms and flowing lines of the costumes and by the profusion of ornamental pattern.

The form of this miniature is conventional for the period; the orderly design is the framework for imaginative presentation of theme. Order and theme are adapted to each other, are fused into a unity. Vertical and horizontal divisions impart tranquility; and this enhances, by contrast, the emotional character of the mourners as expressed by their postures and gestures. The esthetic feeling of the total composition, however, is that of a harmonious unity deriving from the expressive division of the surface area.

In Fig. 3, a gouache miniature of the Indian Kangra School, somewhat later than the Persian, the style is less rigid and the composition considerably less involved than in the Persian painting. But the division of the surface is equally clear. While the geometrical nature of this division is offset by the flowing and curvilinear pattern throughout, there is nevertheless a simplification of the forms in the picture that contributes to the geometrical structure. For instance, the mass of foliage forms a triangle. Further, the figure standing on the left is essentially a rectangle, the peacock fan a simple arc. (For the moment we pass over the imaginative rhythmic elements, which distinguish this School.) Note the use of windows and door as elements in the division of the surface space.

In a very different sector of Oriental art we find an example of rectangular surface division as close to Mondrian's as one is likely to encounter in pictorial art. (Perhaps Mondrian *had* encountered this and similar works.) This is a Japanese print attributed to Shigenobu (Fig. 4). The rectangular spaces that serve as background for the group are skillfully knitted to the group by the use of diagonals. The diagonal in the lower left corner makes an interesting surface division but it also serves to define a rug or mat which, thrusting inward, unites the squatting near figure with the standing one. The head and neck of the right figure are tipped downward and their axis is repeated in the many diagonal lines that divide the rectangle behind. This direction repeats the inward thrust of the rug, so that the edge of the rug is seen in a dual role, as part of a surface rhythm and as a receding edge. Note also how the stripes in the robe of the seated figure spiral into the diagonal lines behind the figure. The depiction of the figures is accomplished through many spirals but these are so tied to the rectangular structure that the viewer is at first unaware of the dissimilar styles of figure and background. It is the orderly setting, the inventive division of the surface that imparts a gracious serenity to the scene. (As in the

Figure 3

Kangra School, *Toilette of Radha*
The Cleveland Museum of Art,
Edward L. Whittemore Fund

Figure 4

Shigenobu, *Three Maidens*

Figure 5

Russian Ikon, *The Purification of the Virgin*. A la Vieille Russie

9

Indian miniature the dark pattern strengthens and enriches the rhythm.)

The instinct and capacity for organization is universal. Although the examples shown are Oriental, there are equally fine examples of surface division in Western art, particularly in early Italian painting. Nor is this capacity limited to these sharply disparate cultures. Consider for example the anonymous Russian icon of the 15th Century (Fig. 5). The charm of this painting derives from the quaint imagery, the Byzantine elongation of the figures, the free interpretation of architectural forms. We first take note of the large space-divisions of the area; then we become intrigued by the smaller shapes of the spaces. Note the patterns of space made by the arches in the center structure, their diversity, and particularly, the inventive patterns that together form the building at the upper right corner. This shapemaking artistry is also apparent in the opposite corner and in the design of the left margin. The organization of the areas throughout is enchanting in its variety and harmonious interplay. In this respect the painting resembles works of Duccio and even of Fra Angelico, though the rather expressionistic drawing, and the imagery generally, is Russian.

Before turning to contemporary modes of division of the surface area we may glance at two remarkably fine examples of European composition, the Sassetta painting of *Saint Anthony Leaving the Monastery* (Fig. 6), and Vermeer's *The Love Letter* (Fig. 7). These are of different centuries, of different cultures. Yet they have in common this quality of orderly division of the surface area. The stark simplicity of the Sassetta makes it unnecessary to point out the division of the surface. The organization of patterns of varying sizes with the large central mass of the facade as nucleus is the essence of order. The composition is particularly noteworthy because it expresses tremendous spatial thrust. This is achieved not only by the sharp perspective of the steps but by the tension created by the dark pattern of the window in the wall on the left, when seen in relation to the dark patterns of arches in the upper right of the picture. The facade of the monastery actually appears to be pushing these dark patterns apart. Yet so well are all the dark shapes placed that the picture when turned on its side presents a rhythmic and balanced pattern that contributes to the orderly division of space.

The Vermeer painting provides an effective contrast in style with the Sassetta. The sharp Italian clarity of the latter is displaced by Northern softness of light and shadow. The edges are blurred. The modulations of tone impart an atmospheric realism (somewhat idealized) that would appear to be the major objective of Northern painting. But in Vermeer's hands verisimilitude and atmosphere are not the ends in themselves. He establishes a mood of calm gentility by the nature of his space-division. It is not just the elegance of draperies and furniture which creates this mood, it is the manner in which they are made into pattern. In this particular work note the importance of the two major areas, the curtain on the left and the large romantic painting on the rear wall.

It has been said frequently that Mondrian is the legatee of the Vermeer tradition. There is no doubt that the serenity and air of immutability in the works of the Dutch master deeply moved the Belgian artist. The word "classical" may be applied equally to both masters of surface division however unlike their art may be in mode, style, and superficial appearance.

Classical traditions of surface division have been kept alive by individual artists through all the changes in Western painting. Compared to the last two examples the appearance or image of a cubist-inspired painting may seem bizarre, but a prolonged look will reveal the same orderly stability. In the case of Roger de la Fresnaye, the orderly stability often becomes nobility—that is to say, the projection of a rare feeling for harmonious relationships. See for example his *View of a Bridge* (Fig. 8). The pictorial elements here are very meager, a row of houses and a small stone bridge. Yet interest derives from the imaginative complexes of pattern within each large area. Strength and subtlety are thus combined.[2]

The contemporary painter oriented toward abstract and non-figurative painting may regard the foregoing examples of surface-area-division as isolated landmarks in a history of representational art and therefore without relevancy to his own work. He may protest that the effort to organize, in the works shown, was made in conjunction with themes, figures, objects, or natural phenomena, none of which concerns him. On the other hand, he cannot accept Mondrian's absolutism precisely because it is so pure and leaves no scope for the artist's fantasy for shapes, let alone his emotional states. It is of course obvious that certain emotional states cannot be expressed through an organized and sub-divided area. But since our interest is at present in the principles and disciplines of painting as a background for many forms of contemporary expression (exclusive of completely automatic or "cathartic" painting) we should like to show examples of surface division by painters of our time engaged in abstract and non-figurative art. We shall see that they adhere to the traditions of other centuries and cultures, not in style or idiom, but in their concern

---

[2] For the space-concept that determined the form of this painting see Chapter 5.

Figure 6

Stefano di Giovanni, called Sassetta,
*Saint Anthony Leaving His Monas-
tery*. National Gallery of Art,
Washington, D.C. Samuel H.
Kress Collection

Figure 7

Jan Vermeer, *The Love Letter*
Collection of Sir Alfred Beit

Figure 8

Roger de la Fresnaye, *View of a Bridge*

for the intelligent organization of the surface areas of their canvases.

A contemporary artist of major stature is the Russian Serge Poliakoff (generally classified as a French abstractionist). Poliakoff's painting is as intensely personal as Mondrian's. It does in fact bear a certain relationship to Mondrian's; it is extremely introspective, detached from all outside influences—what the French term "silent" painting. To some critics like Marcel Brion, it is charged with a religious emotion. If this is so it expresses what Mondrian professed. The divisions of space, too, are as carefully considered in the works of one as in the other. But here the similarity ends. Poliakoff's work, religious or not, does reflect in its sonorous color a restrained passion that arrests the spectator and holds him. The sensitive viewer is charmed not only by the richness and subtlety of color, but by the sensuous feeling for the pigment itself. While these qualities are lost to us in black and white reproduction the nature of the design is clear. Poliakoff once declared that Braque and Picasso had distorted and deformed the world and killed it like a disease and that he was engaged in an inward search for a way to express the "space of the cosmos." [3] It is significant that this mystical artist did not ally himself with any of the rebellious post-war movements that set out to destroy form, but on the contrary based his painting upon structure and organization. His canvases are notable for the simplicity and harmony of pattern in the division of the surface area.

In Poliakoff's *Composition* (Fig. 9), we note at first glance an apparently flat, static, or motionless image of light and dark masses joined in a monumental form. The cutting up of the total surface into patterns normally results in a flat design, like a map. But as we concentrate our attention we discover an interplay of pattern and a continuity of direction made by the edges of pattern. Further, we become aware that a prolonged look at any of the patterns seems to bring them forward. The space-relation shifts. The painter himself stated that all the parts of his compositions are forms, either major or minor, depending upon the focus of the viewer. Such a shifting of space is attained, first, by occasional overlapping, and again by oppositions and repetitions of direction or axis, termed tension.[4] Study for example the central L-shaped pattern imposed on the larger light and dark shapes. The diagonal direction of this shape appears to be taken up by the rounded shape on the extreme right. These two shapes sand-

---

[3] Julien Alvard, author of *Temoignages de l'art Abstrait*, Editions "Art d'aujourd'hui" Boulogne (Seine), 1952.

[4] We shall refer to this principle of tension throughout.

Figure 9

Serge Poliakoff, *Composition 1950*
The Solomon R. Guggenheim
Museum Collection

wich the dark tone between them so that we experience the illusion of
three distinct spatial planes.

In calling attention to the spatial character of Poliakoff's painting our
purpose is to show the manner in which a richly expressive surface and a
complex spatial concept can be presented in a greatly simplified division
of the surface area.

Division of surface may be either static or dynamic. These terms are
used to distinguish works that deliberately avoid movement from those
whose principal characteristic *is* movement. But "static" is not an exact
term; only the symmetrical is completely static and symmetry results in
formal decoration. A quiet, motionless work is only relatively static. Mondrian's concept of art was that its function was to create a pause, a stasis—
a stop in time to enable the spectator to take refuge in a release from
the commotion of life. His order is therefore a stable, quiet one. Poliakoff's,
as already stated, is similar. Other contemporary painters whose regard for
form is paramount are motivated differently. Rather than turning away
from the turbulence of the world about them they strive to express the
movement and dynamism of life. Such a painter is Afro Basaldella, known
as Afro.

Afro is one of a group of younger Italian painters calling themselves *The
Eight*.[5] These painters work in various abstract idioms but no program
animates them. Everything is grist to their mill. They use cubist and
expressionist forms and devices, a great deal of calligraphy, and do not
disdain subject matter. If recognizable objects accidentally appear, they
may build their compositions about them. Afro particularly employs suggestions of images that are evocative and mysterious. (He even invents
titles for his paintings that have meaning, if any, only for himself.) The
active movement of his color planes and lines is contagiously dynamic.

In his painting *For an Anniversary* (Fig. 10), the space-division is most
varied and imaginative. Unlike the previous examples shown, planes and
pattern interlock in cubist fashion. Patterns intersect and overlap. The
calligraphy skips about the shapes, repeating them, but not defining or
delimiting them, and has the effect of enhancing the movement while
enriching the imagery. The distribution of the light shapes is typical of
this painter's genius for achieving a dynamic balance. Although we do not
see the subtlety of his luminous color and remarkable textures, we are
made aware in this reproduction of the artist's method of dividing his

---

[5] Of these, the leader and guiding spirit was the late Renato Birolli.

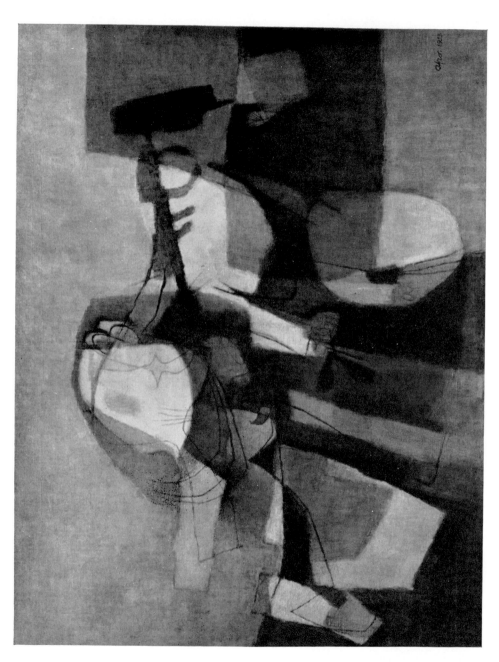

Figure 10

Afro Basaldella, *For an Anniversary,*
1955. The Solomon R. Guggenheim Museum Collection

space, and his personal mode of creating strange and very arresting shapes.

A third type of space-division, quite unlike the two preceding examples, is that of another celebrated abstractionist and non-figurative artist, the late Nicolas de Stael.[6] His painting has had tremendous influence upon a new generation because of its directness, power of statement, imaginative relationship of color, and particularly, his impressive organization of the surface area.

In his painting *Composition on a White Ground* (Fig. 11), we are confronted with a work startlingly different from the consciously designed previous examples. The immediate image is one of laxity and whim— something resembling a child's expression. However, as we study the reproduction we become aware of the existence of certain principles, whether consciously arrived at or not. Among these is the division of the total area into four or five sections. The upper left section is almost blank; the upper right is painted loosely in blocks; the lower right contains some scattered darks—ragged rectangular passages tipped downward; the lower left is a roughly textured surface in which undefined spots, apparently made by swift strokes of a broad brush, are arranged in a somewhat circular pattern. It is the variation in treatment of each area that separates them and imparts an order. The most notable aspect of the painting, we readily see, is its rhythmic distribution of dark spot; we shall have occasion to refer to this later. Here it is the space-division that holds our attention. It is of particular interest in this composition because it underlies an idiom of extreme freedom or abandon generally associated with expressionist painting where one finds little regard for formal principles of any kind. Thus it can be seen that concern for basic structure, such as division of the surface area, is no barrier to the freest or most personal mode of expression.

EXERCISES

The first exercise is based upon the Mondrian concept of vertical and horizontal blocks of color. Cover an area 14″ x 18″ of grained charcoal paper with an even gray tone. Divide the area into approximately fifteen rectangles unlike each other in size and proportion. This division will be facilitated by drawing straight lines in both horizontal and vertical direc-

---

[6] De Stael was a truly international artist, a restless wanderer through many countries. Born in Russia, established for a time in Belgium, then in Paris, he traveled throughout Europe, visited America, and spent some time in Northern Africa. His restless, emotional drive is visible in the intensity and even violence in the application of his color.

Figure 11

Nicolas de Stael, *Composition on White Ground*
Photograph Jacques Dubourg,
Collection Particulière, Paris

tions, from margin to margin, but spaced imaginatively. The intersecting lines will, of course, form blocks or rectangles of varied size. With the kneaded eraser wipe out charcoal tone in three of the blocks, selecting those that will provide a balance without being symmetrical. Then select three other areas for non-symmetrical placing of black tones. The black areas are independent of the white. Each group provides its own non-symmetrical balance (see example, Fig. 12). The remaining gray areas may be varied in value (degree of dark) as shown.

The exercise above may be developed as a painting by translating each black rectangle into a deep color, the three hues roughly equal in value.[7] The white areas should be painted next, each slightly tinted by one of the given hues. All the remaining areas will then be painted in variations of value but always restricted in hue to the original colors chosen. Follow as closely as possible the charcoal version. At the end introduce one note of a new color, as a vivid accent.

Textural effects may be introduced by varying the application of pigment. Painting knife and brush should both be employed. Some areas may be thin and translucent, others heavy and buttery. Manipulation of brush and knife for stippling and scraping, respectively, will provide additional interest. But no technical or textural effects will take the place of a well-balanced and imaginative surface division.

2. A variation of the exercise above is a collage made by a combination of color-printed advertising pages of magazines and a package of construction paper. (This is an assortment of colored sheets of heavy paper sold by artist's materials shops.) Paste up varied rectangles of both, using the more strongly colored construction paper in small areas only for accent. See that no two rectangles are alike in size and give special attention to placing of the three very light and dark areas.

The charcoal drawing, the painting, and the collage will appear rigid and very controlled since this is the nature of the exercise. Freedom lies in the choice of each element of the organization; but not in impulsive expression. The challenge to one's sense of construction may be less exciting than the impulsive pure play experience, but it is our belief that the play experience is fruitful only after the sense of construction and the sense of balance have been explored, if not deeply developed. For this reason it is recommended that the foregoing exercises, particularly the collage, be done more than once.

---

[7] For an explanation of the terms hue and value see Chapter 8—Exploring Color.

Figure 12

Morris Davidson, *Space Division*

3. In this charcoal drawing the division of the surface area is inherent in the theme or subject matter. The setting is the interior of a studio. Very little of the studio itself will appear in the composition since most of the area will consist of white canvases of various proportions and dimensions set on easels at varying heights.

In visualizing this situation it will seem a simple undertaking to place a collection of white rectangles in an area in an interesting arrangement. But the problem is complicated by the factor of plausibility. Not only must the arrangement of disparate sizes be inventive, each canvas on its easel must appear in a convincing position with relation to the others. This is largely achieved by a proper placing of the base of the easel upon which the canvas rests. (The easels will be inverted T's.)

The common mistake in doing this exercise is to begin by drawing a canvas on an easel and then adding another and another, etc. The resulting conglomeration when this course is pursued will be most frustrating. The process of addition is directly contrary to the process of dividing the total surface. The idea is not to begin by illustrating canvases on easels, but by filling the area with horizontal and vertical lines of varied length, and spaced imaginatively. The resulting image is simply that of a collection of line fragments, vertical and horizontal.[8] From this maze or pattern of line it will not be difficult to construct rectangles of different sizes. The procedure is to skip over the surface rather than to add one rectangle to another. (See Diagrams I-a and I-b, in which a fragment of the design is shown.) It is important to check the base of each easel to make sure that the canvas that overlaps another is on the nearer, that is, the lower-based, easel.

The final effect should be one of a diversity of spaces. Not only will the canvases provide this diversity, the spaces around the easels will either contribute to the total effect or defeat it, if monotonous. The spaces remaining on the floor may be broken with cast shadows and the spaces on the rear wall may be divided in some plausible manner by a wall hanging, or other furniture. The drawing may be done in clean line with sharp black pattern or on a gray ground out of which the white areas are picked with a kneaded eraser.

The painting of this exercise is Project 1 described in Chapter 9.

---

8 We are familiar with Mondrian's ruled painting of flat rectangles, but may not be familiar with his freer work in which the total area in monochrome is covered with just such line fragments, spaced imaginatively.

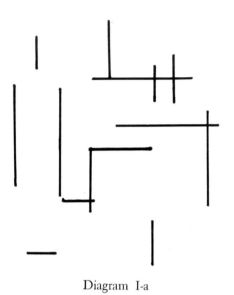

Diagram I-a

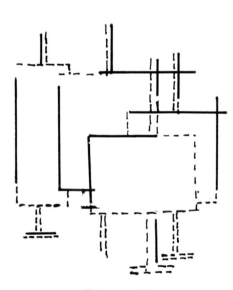

Diagram I-b

4. Let us here assume that the student has demonstrated, at least to his own satisfaction, that he is able to make an interesting space-division without depending upon inventive shapes, and is therefore ready for a free painting experience. Now he will require a good sized canvas, say 24″ x 30″, so that he may not be cramped. Also, it will add to the spontaneity of his expression if he uses, in addition to large brushes, a good flexible painting knife with a blade three inches long.

Mix or select four hues, two warm and two cool. Without using white pigment as a medium, but only turpentine, stain the canvas into five or

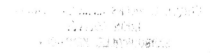

six areas of different shape and size.[9] Since only four colors are used one or two will have to be repeated. Vary the values (degree of light or dark) in the stained areas by deepening some and wiping over others with paint rag. Wipe away sharp edges or boundaries. Now the actual painting begins. With broad strokes of the knife or large brush paint blobs of color somewhat related to the stain in each area. The color may be lighter and darker, less and more intensive, but each blob should be thickly and directly stated without any reworking. (A mauve area may have in it violets and purples, etc.) When firm and varied passages have been distributed in each area without entirely blotting out the stain, distribute a number of very dark notes, black, brown, blue-green, for accent. The essential objective is to control the original areas of color, despite the variations within them, in such manner that the surface will be interestingly divided and balanced.

---

[9] The process of staining the canvas before applying heavy pigment, or pigment mixed with white, has much to recommend it. In the first place it covers the glaring white of the canvas without impairing the canvas weave or "tooth." Then it enables one to explore an idea without committing one's self, since it is relatively easy to wash out an unwanted tone and replace it by another. Again it may be desirable in some parts of the painting for its quality of transparency, as a relief from dense or heavily painted surfaces.

Aside from these esthetic and procedural advantages the stain has the physical or chemical merit of acting as a binder. The author has seen some fine paintings of the twenties in which passages of color have flaked off. In every case the flaking revealed an unstained canvas. In a stained canvas the surface of the priming absorbs the turpentine-diluted color and the thin pigment then will fuse with successive heavier applications.

Distance
and Space

2 The term "representational painting"
covers a wide range of styles and concepts. It embraces
Magic Realism [1] and Surrealism, the neo-primitive, classical
and neo-classical, the romantic and symbolic, and
practically every form of painting in which the subject
matter may be identified. But it also includes the
truly marvelous compositions of early Italian painting and
the painting of Cézanne—painting in which adherence
to concepts overrides naturalistic illusion. Such
painting, while clearly revealing subject matter, has an
underlying structure that is abstract. In fact there is
sometimes more abstraction in sound representational
painting than in much professed abstract art.

At this point we must take a few moments to clarify terms.
The word "abstraction" in painting has different meanings

[1] Magic Realism is a style of painting similar to the photographic still
life of the Dutch. Its intention is to copy nature so accurately and so free
of the artist's technique or brushwork that the spectator will experience
a tactile sensation—a wish actually to touch the objects depicted. It is
trompe l'oeil, a deceiving of the eye.

to different writers and painters. The term as used here may be special but will avoid confusion. The statement of relationships of the various elements in a painting, color, shape, line, value, etc., in a spatial context is here termed abstraction.[2] These relationships may be derived from looking at some situation or collection of things in nature, stressing particular aspects while eliminating others; or the relationships may be invented by the artist so that they appear to have been taken from an actual situation. In each case there is a synthesis, the making of a unity out of the various elements.

When the relationships are such that no link to natural appearance is seen or intended, and no plausible space context defined, the painting is non-figurative or non-objective. For example, the painting of the interior of a box—which we have experienced as the interior of a room, conscious of the space within it—may be abstract. (Villon and Albers have made inventive color compositions of such interiors.) But the painting of similar flat colors in bands or stripes as pure invention, such as Mondrian's, is non-objective.[3]

These several distinctions are made here in the interest of those who are turning from realistic or impressionistic painting to a more creative mode of expression, to greater freedom from literal appearance, to interpretation of relationships in place of recording—in short, to perception.

For the painter without training in the making of such relationships the leap from imitation of appearance into abstract painting (as here defined) can only result in ineptitude, caprice, and confusion. He can plunge into non-figurative *expression* easily enough and do as well as the next person, since in this area only momentary effectiveness is the criterion. But he will derive much greater satisfaction from an understanding of what he is doing. This is possible only through a gradual change in orientation accomplished by exercises designed to re-educate his vision. The first phase in change of vision is the perception of limited space.

"Limited space" requires explanation. It is not the idea of distance,

---

2 "Abstractions are real parts, phases or elements of things, or their relations." Morris R. Cohen, *A Preface to Logic* (New York: Holt, Rinehart & Winston, Inc., 1944), p. 95.

3 Painting which is non-figurative, but which does not seek to express either inventive relationships or a spatial context and which is intended to express feelings or psychological states, is commonly termed Abstract Expressionism. This is a misnomer; it is Expressionism in a non-objective idiom. One phase of such painting has been more properly termed "action painting," since its makers wish to acknowledge that it is a kind of impulsive physical expression without the control of mentally imposed restraints.

the continuous movement from the near into the far. It avoids the infinite, the immeasurable depths, and deals instead with the interrelation of points (or objects) in various positions in a *limited depth*. When we look at a photograph of a landscape we see a gradual diminishing of sharpness, a gradual "fading-out" as we recede into the distance. In the spatial painting no point is so remote that it cannot be made to take its place effectively in the pattern of the surface. The concept of spatial painting is bound up with the division of the surface area, its pattern.

The traditional methods of attaining the illusion of recession into infinity are (1) linear perspective, and (2) atmospheric perspective. In Diagrams II-a and II-b of landscapes we see the conventional methods of each.

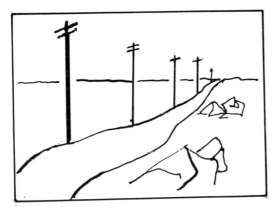

Diagram II-a

Diagram II-b

There are, however, from a contemporary viewpoint, esthetically valid objections to these usages. The unity of the work as division of surface and as rhythmic pattern is destroyed by carrying us from a clearly stated near point to an unexpressed infinite. We have the illusion of looking through a window, of puncturing the canvas surface. It is difficult to imagine a unity made of infinity. From the compositional viewpoint that envisages an over-all balance, there can be no unity if one part has weight, force, and clarity while the other parts of the area are weakly defined. If we turn the diagrams upside down we see at once that there is no intact surface, no picture plane.

This lack of the picture plane is also visible in Diagram II-c, a sketch of city buildings. Here, too, there is distance. In sketch II-d, on the other hand, the buildings are each in front of, or behind, the other; but all contribute

Diagram II-c

Diagram II-d

to the pattern and movement on the surface, as do the clouds in the sky.

So far we have used the word *plane* mainly with reference to the surface of the painting—the picture plane. Since the plane of color is the painter's tool, his language, it would be pertinent at this point to explain its usage more fully.

A plane is, in theory, a flat surface. A flat rectangular mass of color may be used to express a flat surface, but the choice of color will be a determining factor in the position of the flat surface—a position relative to its surroundings. The front of a box is a plane; but the area of space behind the box and the area of space in front of the box are also planes. Now if we substitute a cylinder for a box we see only the top of it as a flat surface. The cylinder, being a rounded form, appears to us in imperceptible gradations of light and shade. The painter who desires to state a situation involving objects and spaces in a consistent and uniform language will not attempt to paint the infinite gradations of light on the rounded surface, but will express it by two flat planes (or possibly three), one for light and one for shade. These two planes taken together will be symbols for roundness. The advantages of this use of flat statement are first, a consistency of idiom and style, and second, an intensified sensation of the actual form. The form is stronger, more positively stated when in planes. (See Diagram II-e.)

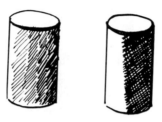

Diagram II-e

In addition to this resolution of appearance into planes, and to the concept of the canvas surface as a picture plane, there is the more complex use of the plane for the construction of the composition. Discussion of this function of the plane must be deferred to the next chapter.

Diagram II-f

Diagram II-g

Diagram II-h

Let us return now to the illusion of depth in the picture. While linear perspective is esthetically and conceptually antagonistic to a unified surface, diagonal thrusts of planes which may, at first glance, resemble perspective, are most useful in creating dynamic movement within the spatial composition. This is particularly true when an opposition of direction (axis) creates a tension. To see how this use of "thrust" enhances the spatial feeling, let us compare the three diagrams II-f, II-g, and II-h. Diagram II-f is a placid arrangement of objects on a flat plane. Diagram II-g shows the same objects distributed at different points spatially. Diagram II-h shows how the spatial differences are intensified by the opposing thrusts of planes.

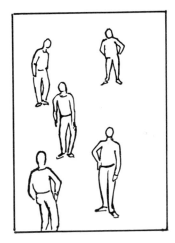

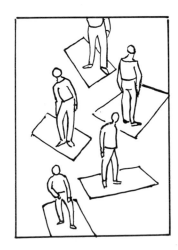

Diagram II-i   Diagram II-j

The effectiveness of opposing thrusts in creating the illusion of recession without recourse to exact or correct perspective and without weakening the picture plane can be graphically demonstrated by showing figures on little islands. In Diagram 11-i perspective is used to illustrate recession; in II-j perspective is not just ignored, it is actually violated by having the farther figures larger and sharper than the nearer ones. Yet they recede and at the same time are part of the surface pattern. It is the alternate change in axis which pushes each island away from the next.

So far we have differentiated the notions of space and distance. But we have not yet concerned ourselves with that special usage generally termed "space-painting," a concept exemplified in some Italian primitive painting and more particularly in cubist and post-cubist art. Such painting can have meaning only when the painter has had some experience in creating limited, related space, and as a consequence has come to reject simple third-dimensional recession. As preparation for a more abstract approach [4] it would be desirable to explore the use of color, value, and plane thrusts to express plausible situations. By intelligent management of these elements, by a set of principles, it is possible to create a spatial representational painting. This is a logical step to abstraction.

EXERCISES

1. The first exercise is a schematic, simplified still life. Imagine a small rectangular table in the corner of a room. On its surface are three objects, a cone, a cylinder, and a box or cube. Each of the objects is placed on a different level, spatially. We are looking down on the table—it is somewhat below eye level—so the nearest object will be the lowest.

We are to paint this situation in flat planes of color. In order to make each part of the painting equally forceful, so that the surface pattern, on its completion, will be immediately apparent, we must use the device of contrast in value (dark and light) opposed to contrast in color (warm and cool). If we made the nearest object and area most forceful and sharpest, as in a photograph, the rest would diminish and fade away. To avoid this we shall reserve our lightest and clearest color for the middle area of the table instead of for the foreground. To begin with, we divide the table into three spatial areas, near, middle, and far, as in Diagram II-k. Note that these areas are not parallel bands. The tone we have selected for the

---

[4] The space-relation in its varied and complex forms is the subject of Chapters 5 and 6.

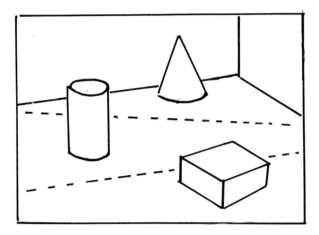

Diagram II-k

light, bright middle area is warm in hue, the color of sand or raw pine. On this area we situate an object, let us say a cylinder. We paint the cylinder in the two flat planes of vivid color, the light side warm and light, the shadow side cool *but also light*. The far area of the table is next. We paint this area cool in hue, not much darker than the warm tone of the middle area. In it we place another object, a cone. This, too, is divided into two planes, but in this instance the warm and cool tones are less vivid in color but stronger in their light and dark contrast. The strength of this value contrast will give as much power to the cone as the cylinder possesses. In the near area the table will be darker but more neutral in color, rather brownish. The cube or box will be painted in flat planes of color, like the rest, but this time mostly neutral in hue, almost black and white. The two walls forming an angle in the background should be strong enough in value and color to hold their place in the surface pattern and thus balance the rest of the painting. It will add to the total pattern to divide these walls into small areas by leaning another object such as a picture frame or magazine against the larger wall. The objective of this exercise, if it requires re-stating, is to situate each object in its space-plane plausibly and convincingly, *while not diminishing the effectiveness of any area.* When turned upside down the painting should, through its controlled contrasts either of color or value, present a unified surface.

2. This exercise consists of six large rectangular areas, like theatre flats or screens, distributed about a room. Construct an interior showing con-

siderable floor, little ceiling, a wall in the rear facing us, and a right and
left wall of different widths. One of these side walls is to be black, or
nearly black. Against this dark wall lean a screen, against the opposite side
wall, two screens, one overlapping the other. In front of the rear wall are
two screens, slightly tipped, also overlapping and not parallel to each

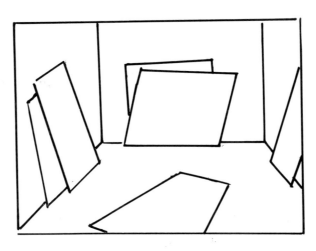

Diagram II-1

other. On the floor, which is painted in three color areas (as in the first
exercise), lies another screen thrusting diagonally inward. All screens,
with the exception of the one lying on the floor, must be plausibly drawn
so that the bottom edge rests on the floor near the walls, to appear to lean
against the walls. For the sake of the pattern avoid parallelism by slight
tipping where one screen overlays another (see Diagram II-1). The problem
is: (1) to paint each area in flat color, that is, without gradations, given
black as one of the areas; (2) to state plausibly the position of each screen;
(3) to make the floor recede by distinct divisions of color; (4) to give
sufficient strength to the rear wall so that it will not fall far back, appearing to be at the end of a bowling alley. The test of the exercise is that
it be vivid in color, equally strong in every part, and possess limited space.
The illusion of space in an interior so painted will be strongly felt, yet
when the canvas is turned on end, or upside down, it should present a
strong color pattern of a well-divided surface area.

3. The third exercise will present little difficulty after the experience with the preceding two. Here we create an interior, mostly a curtained window and a sill on which some object is placed, perhaps a potted plant. In the room there is a piece of furniture, or part of it. Through the window can be seen some architectural forms, a church steeple, or industrial forms, or foliage forms; or even a waterfront scene with masts and sails visible. Control the color so that the interior is definitely separated from the exterior. But design the shapes, line directions, and values in such manner that outdoors and indoors are brought into a fusion on the surface when the canvas is turned upside down.

The preservation of the picture plane, the result of limiting the space, in some cases "telescoping" the space, is the first requisite for a shift in vision from the imitative to the creative. It makes possible a freer expression, the making of a more spirited organization, a synthesis.

Making
a Synthesis

3   One may see on the walls of museums
much undeniably fine painting whose positive qualities are
those of performance. Such painting may be most charming,
magical in execution, or expressive of the painter's keen
insight into character. The painting of a head by Sargent,
for instance, may be a work of great virtuosity with little
dependence for its artistic merit upon the large blank
areas surrounding it. The natural talent and highly developed
skill, the "handwriting," are not attributes that concern us
here. They are the attributes of the performer, not those
of the formative painter, the composer.

The student of painting composition is very differently
motivated from the performer. His special aim is to be in the
stream of art, to paint with the principles of other times
and cultures but at the same time to employ the idiom
of his own day and to reflect the intellectual attitudes of
his own day. To achieve this aim he must exclude or
minimize certain aspects of painting expression such as
virtuosity, sensational effects, sentimentality and

idealization, story-telling or literary characterization. He must concentrate upon the form of the painting, the making of a synthesis out of elements that properly belong to painting—color, shape, space-relation, rhythm, etc. This requires a shift in mental focus from descriptive picturization, and from dramatic effects, to perception of relationships.

Let us turn to the art of drawing as a means of grasping more easily the differences that set apart skilled, accurate statement from dramatic or literary expression; and both of these modes from the making of a rhythmical synthesis.

The draughtsman intent on accurate and skillful description does not look for interesting or novel configurations that shift one's interest away from the thing described. For him the *thing* is the thing; all else is of little significance. He cultivates exactness of observation. To impart an esthetic merit to the keenness of his vision he develops great artistry in technique. There are many remarkably fine Renaissance draughtsmen in this category.

A very different kind of artist is the robust draughtsman of the last century, for example in the style of Daumier. This realist-romanticist also wishes to describe, but even more to characterize. He enjoys drawing for its spontaneous, free-flowing suggestion and exaggeration, rather than for its fine accuracy. His art is muscular and spirited. He does not draw to delight us with the fineness and variety of his line or to give us objective information, but rather to show us how he reacts, or to tell us what he thinks and feels about the thing he is looking at.

A third type of draughtsman neither copies accurately what is before him or scribbles impulsively and exuberantly. His mode of expression is less a matter of technical skill and more a matter of flexible adjustment to his rhythmic sensibility. He is selective rather than objective. He experiences pleasure not in the physical or muscular act of drawing but in putting down hidden relationships which he has discovered. While style as an end in itself is not his concern he strives to combine—through variation of pressure, thickness and thinness, scratchiness and suavity—fragments of line to make configurations that are in themselves esthetically arresting. But above all his aim is to make a unity in which each part is dependent upon the rest.

These differences in modes of drawing will be apparent when we look at the three portrait drawings reproduced. These are: a charcoal study by Holbein (Fig. 13), an etching by Beckmann (Fig. 14), and an ink and brush sketch by Gaudier-Brzeska (Fig. 15). In the first we admire the

Figure 13

Hans Holbein, *Frau mit Haube*
Staatliche Museen, Berlin

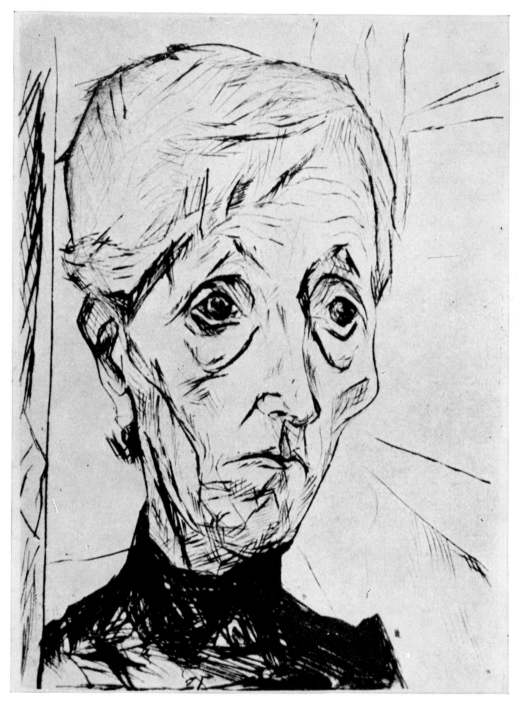

Figure 14

Max Beckmann, *Etching: Head of a Woman*

Figure 15

Henri Gaudier-Brzeska, *Head of Ezra Pound*

sensitive line and faultless execution which has captured the most subtle variations of facial contour. Artistry in execution is the essence. In the second drawing, that of Beckmann, we have a sketchy, slightly distorted impression of an old lady. Here the characterization is subjective, it has the impact of exaggerated statement and is in essence literary—that is to say it does not move us greatly esthetically, by its style, as the Holbein does, but by its commentary; it reveals to us the *pathetic disintegration* of old age. In Gaudier-Brzeska's sketch of Ezra Pound we see an entirely different intention of the artist. With an Oriental economy of brush strokes he makes use of a few simple motifs and configurations and puts them together to make a rhythmic pattern. Instead of subjective characterization there is a keen searching, a discovery of motifs, of esthetic elements. Yet these elements strongly identify the subject. This is perception. The assembling of such elements is a rhythmic synthesis.

With this introduction let us now turn to three charcoal drawings that do not presume to match the artistry of those described but that are nevertheless related *conceptually* to the portraits. These are simple fragments of a still life set-up (Fig. 16). The first is a relatively correct and clean description of a jug and bottle set against a tipped card. It reveals careful observation and is conscientiously if not sensitively stated. The second is an evocative impression, very free and spirited, but not committed to specific statement. The third is of an entirely different character from the other two, principally in its shift of interest from the *things* to the *interrelationships*. The line is used (1) to find continuities, to unite; (2) to create an abstract rhythm.

To draw with this rhythmical interest is particularly difficult for one accustomed to loose sketching in scribbly fashion. But the abstract manner of seeing, of perceiving, is an even more difficult accomplishment. There is a mistaken notion that abstract structure and organization are the result of a drawn-out process of gradual states in the "freeing" of one's self from the photographic image. Some years ago a motion picture was made of Picasso's manner of reaching an abstraction by a series of progressive modifications. First he made a literal copy of his model and then proceeded to make re-statements, each more abstract than the previous one. This was excellent entertainment. But this method has done a great deal of harm in that it makes it appear that perception is not really the act of perceiving but is merely a trick. Such a process is easy for Picasso; no doubt he delighted in showing his resourcefulness in converting commonplace imagery to inventive and provocative shapes. But in so doing he revealed his clever-

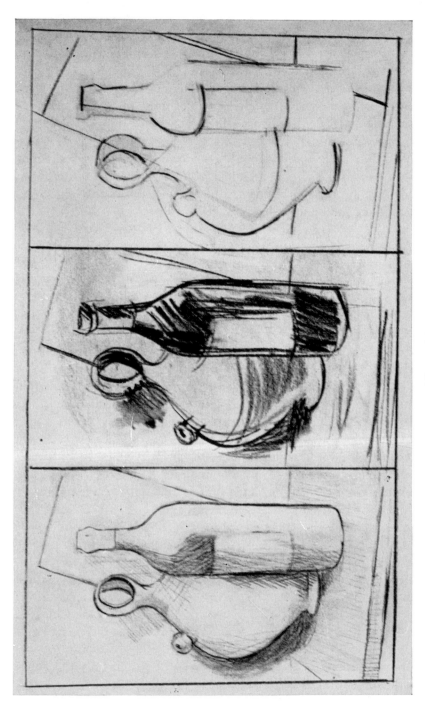

Figure 16

Morris Davidson, *Three Versions of*
Still Life Fragment

45

ness and experience rather than an actual process, or his own way of responding to visual stimulus. Psychologically, the idea of beginning with the literal image and transforming it in stages is a destructive one since it never releases the painter from the literal view of surrounding phenomena. *The very attribute which differentiates the vision of the artist is his perceptive way of seeing.* This is what is meant by the term "the painter's eye."

With the foregoing distinctions between the several modes and motivations in drawing clarified, it should be less difficult to discover similar tendencies in the art of painting. Further, the idea of a synthesis should have a more precise meaning.

A synthesis is an organization of all the parts of the canvas to make a unified, interrelated whole. But a distinction must be made between a synthesis which is serenely stable and architectural, like Mondrian's rectangles, and one in which the movement is compelling.

There has existed in art from earliest times this opposition of the static and the dynamic. To some artists such as Mondrian, and to some cultures such as the ancient Egyptian, the function of art was to provide a serene and contemplative pause in the meaningless hurly-burly of life. To other artists and cultures the function of art has been to express the rhythm of nature (Chinese), the exuberance and joy of life (Indian), and the religious emotion (Byzantine). The methods and modes of expressing such active principles are most varied. We recall, for instance, paintings by El Greco in which a dynamic movement through the canvas is attained by flashing tongues of light. A mysterious force, almost electrical, permeates his work. We term it strongly rhythmical. But equally rhythmical are very different works which generate or express grace or playful lyricism—which do not appear to be, at first glance, dynamic. Such is the painting of the Florentines of the Renaissance. The rhythmic line of Botticelli is too well known to require illustration.

Another resource of the painter for affecting the viewer, for making him respond to an active principle in the painting, is the skillful distribution of shapes and spots. This is the special province of the Chinese and Japanese artists to whom a mastery of rhythm of this mode is a requisite for the career of artist. This we have seen in the Japanese print reproduced in the first chapter (Fig. 4, p. 8), in which the patterns of black intensify the rhythm of the calligraphic line.

Before venturing upon the experience of making a synthesis let us give some attention to an analysis of a modern representational work. By dis-

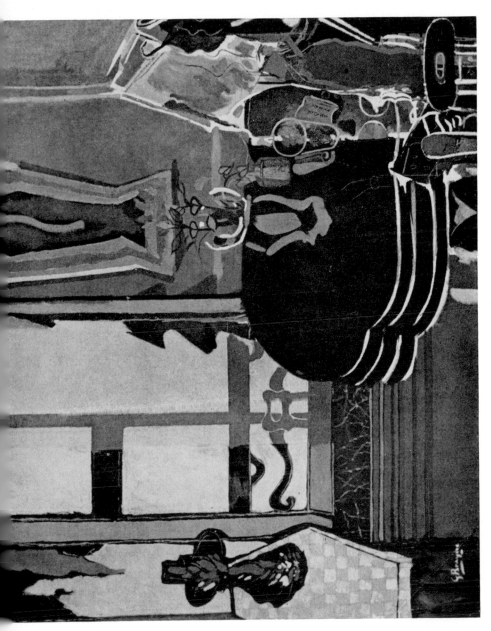

Figure 17

Georges Braque, *Le Salon*. Musée
National d'Art Moderne, Paris

47

covering what goes into the making of a composition we shall be better prepared to put together one of our own.

Figure 17 is a reproduction of a painting by Georges Braque, *Le Salon*. At first glance we note the division of the surface. The spaces are clearly defined. The painting appears to be a flat, well-balanced design. There is no illusion of recession over the table surface or the surface of the chest on the left. Yet we do experience a differentiation in space between the window and the objects on the table. The method by which this difference is achieved is the overlapping of planes. The rounded plane of the table projects over the rectangle of the window, the chest projects over the left window frame, the diagonal rectangles on the extreme right project over the rear walls, the chair in the foreground projects over the front edge of the table. With all this overlapping there is a continuity of vertical and horizontal movements that impart a placid order and unity. We then become aware of the shapes. There is a stylistic character to the shapes that stamps them as the personal idiosyncrasy of the painter. Compare, for example, the shapes in the upper left corner with those on the right lower edge of the window, and with the vase on the black tablecloth. But note also that these spontaneous shapes are offset by consciously designed shapes both positive and negative,[1] such as those at the bottom of the window, under the table, and on the right margin.

One other resource of the painter is the linear pattern. In this painting line is a vital factor in creating a movement that offsets the placid structure. The lower right part of the painting particularly is most active in its calligraphy. Our gaze is swept around by the four parallel lines of the tablecloth, caught in a maze of arabesques, and taken upward. This spirited movement then is picked up in the heavy ornamental pattern at the bottom of the window.

The total significance of the painting is of course lost to us without the color. Even a color reproduction is not the same thing as the painting wherein the pigment itself speaks to us. But for the purpose of learning to put elements together, it is useful to learn to take them apart. It is for this reason that we say nothing of the charm, the feeling, the poetry of vision, and the expression.

---

[1] Respectively the shapes representing some thing or substance, and the spaces between or around these shapes.

EXERCISES

1. One should begin by first gaining control of the charcoal. Use vine charcoal (pointed hard charcoal is unsuited to free drawing). Place the charcoal loosely in the hand (as in Diagram III-a) allowing about an inch

Diagram III-a

to project above the forefinger. Rest the hand lightly on the paper. Practice drawing long vertical lines by starting at the top of the sheet and allowing the arm to drop. The tendency will be to lift the hand away from the paper; but if this is done, control will be lost. After vertical lines are mastered, draw diagonal lines, this time with a swinging motion of the arm, then curved lines, etc. But keep in mind that the charcoal should never be pushed (or held at a right angle to the line direction); it should be pulled into the direction wanted. A flexible wrist and a free swinging arm are essential to clean, rapid statement.

When control of the charcoal is achieved by keeping the backs of the fingers upon the paper at all times then it is possible to make clean statement of line relationship, straight, curved, and fluid, of varied pressure and thickness.

2. Set up a still life group and explore in charcoal various configurations of line for an over-all linear pattern rather than to describe objects. The photograph (Fig. 18) shows a still life arrangement; Diagram III-b is a structural line drawing in which the essential lines are freely but cleanly stated. (The drawing was of course made from the set-up, not from the photograph.)

3. Having tried several interpretations of the still life set-up, the draughtsman-painter will then attempt to create a still life by putting together the various elements given. The intention is to create a rhythmic synthesis out of these elements.

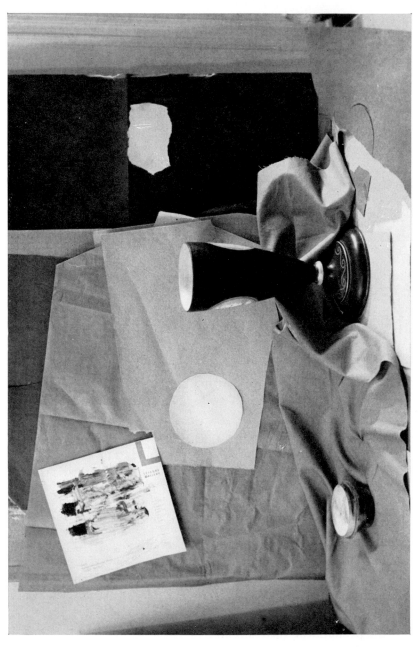

Figure 18

Morris Davidson, *Photograph of Still Life*

Diagram III-b

Acquired control of the charcoal is first put to use in the drawing of a line expressing great motion, like the crack of a whip. This line should be diagonal in its axis and varied in each bend or curve, that is, different in size and shape (Diagram III-c). If the line is slowly and carefully constructed it will not have the quality of action required; it must be drawn with great rapidity. Cover the surface of a large newsprint pad with a number of such lines, working from the upper left corner of the line to the lower right. (Avoid making lines with a vertical axis.) In other words, pull the charcoal downward and to the right in rapid S patterns. When the lines begin to be free and varied, convert them into scrolls by the addition of near-vertical lines, as in Diagram III-d.

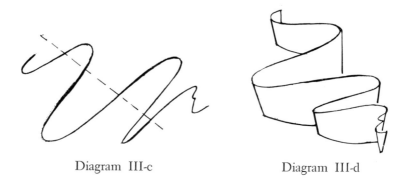

Diagram III-c   Diagram III-d

4. Now turn to another calligraphic invention. This time attempt to depict two pears in a continous line, rapidly drawn, making it appear that one is slightly in front of the other (Diagram III-e). Cover a newsprint sheet with different calligraphic images of the two pears. Then try to unite the two by a round black spot where one overlaps the other.

5. On newsprint 18″ x 24″, with three lines construct the corner of a table in the corner of a room (Diagram III-f). Draw a rectangular card lying diagonally on the table, its top edge somewhat to the right, its bottom edge to the lower left. On top of this card place a standing scroll running in the opposite direction from the card. Place calligraphic pears on the table. Divide the larger wall area by drawing a book or card leaning slightly diagonally against it.

6. Using the black spot of the pears as a point of departure, distribute other shapes of black throughout the area, giving careful attention to variety of shape and size, and most particularly, to variety in the spacing between black patterns, the interval. All the line drawing in the composi-

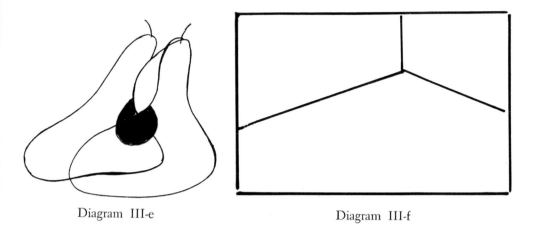

Diagram III-e   Diagram III-f

tion should be light and crisp except the calligraphic line of the top of
the scroll and the line of the pears. These stressed lines together with the
black pattern will create rhythmic movement. Their function is not to
describe or convey information; it is rather to express a spirited or playful
impulse. As such it is an element of an abstract synthesis.

To translate such a drawing into a painting by copying it onto the canvas
is not advisable; such a procedure would be in the nature of an illustration.
Having made several drawings reversing the directions of table, card, and
scroll, and having tried various positions for the pears, the student should
discard his drawings and begin painting with stains of color at random.
He should approach the canvas freshly, with no pre-conceived plan. He
will paint warm-white and cool-white passages, without defining their shape,
in the general area where the scroll will appear. He will put down a dull,
or olive green block of color where the pears are to appear. The card will
be suggested (but not defined) by variations of a vivid hue. The background
will be an improvisation of colors. When all the canvas has been covered
the calligraphic lines will be imposed, the directions of card and table
subtly indicated. Then the total picture will be studied for its balance.
The light areas of the scroll will be echoed elsewhere. Dark pattern or
accent will be distributed non-symmetrically. Vivid small notes of color
may be added to enhance the rhythmic movement. Shapes may be designed
in the background to enhance, by contrast, the effectiveness of the scroll.
The total impression should be one of vital movement and not merely the
colored replica of a worked-out drawing. The production of such a painting
of movement is the making of a rhythmical synthesis.

Interpretation
of the
Landscape

4   While a great many books have been
written on the art of landscape painting, they have in the
main been concerned with traditional picture-making
before Cézanne. The word *landscape* itself calls to mind the
long history of scene painting of many schools, classical
and romantic. It would seem irrelevant, therefore, to discuss
this phase of painting in connection with contemporary
aspirations and forms of painting. The only reason for
doing so is that many painters, variously abstract, still take
their point of departure, if not their inspiration, from nature.
Without wishing to express mood or poetic sentiment or
idealization, they search out those aspects of the scene
that will afford them material for an inventive composition.
The contemporary painter does not give us a report or
description of a scene, or a poetic mood, but rather an
interpretation. He makes a synthesis more or less
evocative of a place and of the forms discoverable in it.

    Such a synthesis bears a relation to the synthesis
outlined in the previous chapter, the making of a still life

composition. Its essential nature, we recall, was the creation of a unified, rhythmic situation invested with objects. In going to the landscape the creative painter is similarly motivated, except that he is more concerned with spaces than with things. (We are here speaking of the visual essence of the landscape, not of the items, trees, grass, earth, etc., that are to be found in it.) The problem of the contemporary landscapist is, then, like that of the still life painter, one of perception. He must take from the scene aspects that lend themselves to his purpose. Where the spaces are visible through the pattern, as for example the pattern of a ploughed field against a pattern of hills behind it, the landscape is paintable; where there is no such differentiation of areas there is little to work with regardless of descriptive detail. With this difference taken into account, namely the difference between discovering relationships in limited space and relationships over vast areas, the problem of perception remains the same.

Very few painters today work out of doors. Some will make quick sketches in casein or gouache to "get the feel of a place," or just for the pleasure sketching affords. But serious composition is done in the studio. The advantages of working in the studio are obvious. The difficulty of transporting equipment able to accommodate a large canvas is in itself an obstacle. But aside from physical drawbacks there is the more serious handicap of being dominated by the colors and tones of nature. Such dominance stifles the imagination, shifts the painter's intentions from the unity of his work to a kind of idealized mimetism. This the imaginative painter zealously avoids.

There are some painters who believe that perception in this technological age is obsolete. Their method is to bring their cameras to the scene to do their preliminary work. This practice is much more common than one would suppose. The assumption is that one can abstract from a color photograph as well as from nature. But it is a mistaken assumption because it implies that the process of abstraction is merely a formula for transforming descriptive images into unrecognizable or distorted shapes. The element of personal discovery is eliminated by the mechanical eye. Psychological response to visual stimulus is bypassed. In place of discovery and response, in place of a visual experience, the camera landscapist attempts to transform a prettified two-dimensional impersonal image into an "abstraction." Needless to say such abstraction is at best only clever contrivance.[1]

---

[1] The objections raised in the previous chapter to the Picasso film in which he shows successive stages of abstraction are as pertinent here.

Figure 19

Morris Davidson, *Ink Sketch of Landscape*

The method followed by most contemporary painters is to go to the scene with pencil and pad. When the selection of a site has been made based upon possibilities for pattern, an abstract line synthesis follows. This of course is in clean sharp line without any pictorial rendering, limited to the play of one line against another. Such lines are abstracted from visible demarcations in the scene. The major lines will establish the structure of the composition. These may be the contours or edges of a field, a stone wall, a range of hills, a bridge, or a stream. After setting down the major lines, smaller line fragments will be added, not for descriptive purposes but to enhance the movement and vary the interest. The constructive sense of the draughtsman is expressed in the manner in which he relates straight line to curve and rippling or wavy line to angle. The completed drawing should present interesting configurations even when turned upside down or on its side. (See sketch, Fig. 19).

Some practical suggestions may be in order. A suitable pad for outdoor pencil drawing is a 9″ x 12″ spiral-bound sketch pad with board covers. An ordinary No. 2 pencil is adequate, and a pencil eraser indispensable. In beginning the drawing it is advisable to make a half-inch margin on the paper. It is difficult to prove the assertion that such a margin will insure a better drawing, but experience has shown that it has the psychological effect of making the draughtsman aware of edges and the shapes within corners. In other words, it unconsciously focuses attention upon the design. When the line pattern fits well within the margin the spacing will be of help to the painter when the drawing is transferred to canvas.

The linear movement described is not the only preparation for the landscape painting. On other pages of the pad, the special items in the scene will be drawn cleanly and descriptively. Whether it be a church tower, stone fence, a fishing trawler, or whatever complicated object, clean line drawings should describe their construction fairly accurately. Even if only three line fragments taken from such drawing are used in the composition they can appear to be authentic. Nothing so destroys the landscape painting as an impossibly constructed object built out of one's faulty memory. (How many harbor scenes have been ruined by absurdly constructed fishing boats!) It is better to resolve the object into a simple block of color, or triangle, than to call attention to the ineptness of the artist or to his lack of perception. The value of the careful notations, then, is as material for later reference, to supplement, where considered necessary, the original line pattern made from the scene. This work is done in the studio by copying the first pencil drawing onto the charcoal pad and then introducing into this drawing such descriptive reference material as deemed desirable for interest; perhaps only enough as is necessary to convey the flavor of the locale. In an abstract landscape even one authentic symbol may be enough.

An example of such restriction to one descriptive note is a well known water color of Paul Klee, *Kairouan* (Fig. 20). It consists of rectangular blocks, most of them variations of sand color. Above these blocks of warm tone are a few line fragments describing or rather symbolizing mosques. These are the only lines in the picture. The watercolor is given the name of an Arab desert village in North Africa and conveys the sense of place with startling effect.

It is apparent to the reader that the kind of landscape painting we are concerned with is more or less abstract. But how abstract should the interpretation be? This is a question best left to individual taste. For the

Figure 20

Paul Klee, *Kairouan*
© *Cosmopress* and *Spadem* by
French Reproduction Rights Inc.,
1963

student with little experience in this field a point worth keeping in mind is that the painting should at least evoke a sense of place, of a particular locale. Otherwise it could just as well be an invented composition without the preliminary work of drawing on the scene.

It would seem that a practical method of interpreting the pencil drawing or the charcoal drawing made from it would be to copy it onto the canvas and proceed to fill in color areas from memory. But such a method generally results in a pedestrian performance. A better plan is one similar to the free painting exercise described in Chapter 1. Stain the canvas with a few large color patterns based loosely upon the divisions indicated by the long lines of the drawing. Then begin the painting with thin passages of color without any definition or descriptive purpose. When these passages begin to form an interesting combination of tones, the charcoal drawing is more carefully studied. The long lines will permit the making of pattern. They may be boldly drawn over the canvas or lightly indicated, depending upon the style of the work. The composition will depend upon these rhythmically important lines. The pencil notations of interesting detail will be studied to see which might contribute to the special character of the scene. Beyond this the major effort will be directed to making a synthesis, a rhythmical unit, inventive in color, and non-symmetrically balanced.[2]

Styles in contemporary landscape painting are apt to be highly personal. Plastic principles are easily emphasized in this art. Spatial tensions that arise from opposing thrusts are clearly visible in rolling country. Spiral and curved contours of roads and trees and clouds create rhythm. Opportunities for inventive pattern abound. Color may be as unhackneyed and as fanciful as one's imagination permits since the moods of nature are unpredictable. To show extreme divergences in concept and style we reproduce two works, one by that most plastic of painters, Roger de la Fresnaye, the other by the lyrical British landscapist Ivon Hitchens.

Fresnaye's painting *Landscape at Meulan* (Fig. 21) is a model of space-organization (as are most of this artist's paintings). The composition is built of opposing diagonal thrusts relieved by the spherical forms of trees

---

[2] It is of course possible to resolve the drawing from the scene into a few broad areas of color, in which case the painting becomes a complete abstraction. This is the method that de Stael employed. It is questionable, however, whether a landscape so abstracted can evoke the feeling of nature more strongly than one which develops as a synthesis, and imaginatively, without any reference to a scene at all but out of an organization of planes or patterns of color. This each painter must find out for himself. (Project No. 7 in Chapter 9 involves such a process.)

Figure 21

Roger de la Fresnaye, *Landscape at
Meulan*. The Collection of Mr. and
Mrs. Ralph F. Colin, New York

and clouds. Each plane is clearly situated with relation to the others. Yet all combine to produce a surface pattern of harmonious shapes. Dynamic movement and the serene comfort of rounded forms interact to provide us with a most agreeable and orderly view of nature (and of the artist's spirit).

In Hitchens' painting entitled *Mill Pool, Blue Gray Afternoon* (Fig. 22) we see a very different esthetic attitude. Abstraction of space is not his concern. The landscape for this artist appears to be a stimulus to his rhythmic sensibility rather than to his sense of construction. (When forms are dissolved into swift passages of color, structural planes are necessarily eliminated.) But the painting is lyrical because of its linear rhythm. Moreover, the impulsive technique, its dash and economy of effort, are consonant with the spirit of present-day free expression.

Figure 22

Ivon Hitchens, *Mill Pool, Blue Grey
Afternoon, 1950*
Courtesy of the artist

The
Space-Relation
and
Architectonic
Space

5   In an earlier chapter we touched on
the illusion of distance and the painting of limited space.
In describing the esthetic advantage of the latter type of
painting, stress was laid upon its dual nature. We see objects
or points behind or in front of each other; we experience a
movement of color backward and forward. But simultaneously
(provided we shift our focus) we become aware of a surface
pattern, a rhythm which tends to unite disparate spaces
on the picture plane. This we observed in a rather
simplified demonstration, the illustration of the buildings
in Chapter 2, Diagram II-d.

The ingenuity with which certain celebrated artists have
achieved such simultaneous illusions might be the subject
of a separate volume. From Italian Primitive and early
Renaissance through Hindu and Persian painting,
in Japanese prints and Chinese scrolls, from Poussin to
Cubism, examples of this fusion of depth and
surface, accomplished by varied and ingenious means and
devices, may be found. Not only is there this shift in position

from depth to surface, but there exist, from the earliest periods of painting, examples of an overlapping and interplay of areas of space.

Aside from the esthetic reasons for such interplay, namely the greater sense of unity attained by the shifting of spaces with reference to the surface, and the appeal of the surface pattern, there is another element, a psychological one, that underlies the esthetic. This is the sense of magic, the phenomenological, or simply the poetic.

The creation of poetic illusions is precisely the objective of the space painter. Just as factual reporting, however poetically written, does not yield poetic mystery, so a naturalistic rendition of things in fixed position, however poetically stated, does not allow for the multiple (and magical) possibilities of a complex space-relation. Courbet and Fra Angelico, for instance, lived in different worlds, the one seeking factual truth, the other a more subjective reality. The first was a conscientious reporter of the scene before him, the second a poetic conjurer of spatial effects.

The concept of space relativity in an architectural structure is sometimes termed architectonic space. One or two examples of its use in early Italian painting will show that it is not at all a recent invention. Let us look for example at Sassetta's *Recognition of the Franciscan Order* (Fig. 23), painted five centuries ago. The figures in this scene create a horizontal block or plane in the foreground, a vertical plane on the left, and a diagonal inward-thrusting plane on the right. This compact grouping is part of a larger plane arrangement of the total area. Here we observe the long rectangle of four-fifths of the canvas facing us and, cutting into it, the diagonal thrust of the plane created by pillars and overhead beam. The vertical right wall and horizontal ornamental block below the seated figures effectively counteract this inward thrust, imparting a structural stability to the painting. Opposition of these two planes, the frontal and the inward-thrusting, is skillfully resolved by the carefully placed ornamented windows that form part of a surface pattern with other ornamented areas. Observe how the downward-thrusting plane at the top, in the circular opening of the frame, accentuates the inward thrust below.

Sassetta's painting is as simple a demonstration of the fusion of opposing planes as can be found. A much more complex organization is Ambrogio Lorenzetti's *View of a City* (Fig. 24). The outside walls of the city create a configuration of harmonious proportions. But they are at the same time involved in a series of multiple relationships. (Diagram V-a shows some of these.) It cannot be said that such complex involvements are accidental, because the artist has obviously stressed parallel lines as, for example, below

Figure 23

Stefano di Giovanni, called Sassetta,
*The Pope Accords Recognition to
the Franciscan Order.* The National
Gallery, London

the castle in the upper right, running these lines through pavement and wall to establish a converging diagonal thrust. So much is made of plane intersection that the lower left wall appears to be done in cubist fashion.

Particular interest in this composition centers in the use of areas or planes in dual spatial context. If we look at the center rectangular form that occupies a third of the architectural mass we unite the nearest wall to one of the tall buildings in the rear by a glance upwards along the left edge of the wall. In the same way we see that the farthest castle, at the top of the painting, appears to be a continuation of the right wall nearest to us. This painting is a remarkable example of dynamic opposing thrusts held together in an architectural structure of great serenity.

From the two foregoing examples we see that there is nothing really new in the spatial concept of the Cubists. But the Cubists must be credited for reviving an interest in this imaginative and magical element of painting. Space relation is accomplished by planes, and Cubism is a textbook of plane involvement. Even though the *ism* is dead as a style its lessons remain alive, animating the art of many distinguished contemporaries. It is therefore pertinent to give some attention to the changes in the usages of space as exemplified by two or three of its foremost exponents and followers.

Lorenzetti's *View of a City* and Fresnaye's *Bridge* (Fig. 8, p. 14), while totally dissimilar technically, have in common the concept of simultaneous thrust and surface pattern. Turning back to Fresnaye's painting we note the strong recessive movement of the block of houses, but this thrust inward

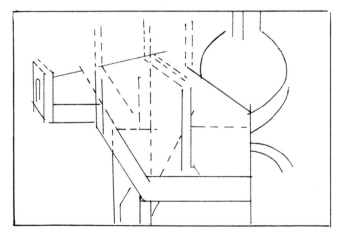

Diagram V-a

Figure 24

Ambrogio Lorenzetti, *View of a City*. Photo Alinari

is sandwiched between the dark of the trees and the heavy dark horizontal line below. The line carries out the horizontal movement of the long roof. The two arches of the bridge are counteracted by the two diagonal planes under them and these in turn are intersected by an arbitrary pattern of light and shadow making roughly a parallelogram with a different axis. The heavy angular rhythms add to the surface design.

A very clear example of a tightly knit spatial structure is Juan Gris' *Le Canigou* (Fig. 25). No section of this painting is completely detached from the rest. In addition to the thorough interlocking of objects (such as the unified mass of pear, guitar, and fruit bowl) there is an interlocking of objects with surrounding space (as for example the left plane of the table surface cutting through the guitar). While the fusion of space and thing is complete this unity is contradicted by dynamic movements, the thrusts of planes in opposing diagonal axes. The table surface, for example, thrusts upward to the left taking with it the ellipse of the bowl; exaggerated perspective intensifies the thrust. But dynamic movement toward the upper left is opposed in the left half of the table by a serene vertical plane reaching from top to bottom, and by a much more forceful plane moving to the upper right, beginning at the bottom right of the table and moving through the block or door in back of the table. This diagonal force, too, is a continuous movement from the bottom to the top of the composition.

In Gris' invention the element of magic derives from the dual spatial position of the major areas. Near and far are in one aspect clearly distinguishable; in another they are fused into a unity. Further, when we squint our eyes we see a light mass uniting diverse spaces into a monumental pattern. This pattern and the block-like vertical left edge of the canvas impart a classical stability to an involved dynamic structure.

Although cubist in concept, Gris' painting is distinctly personal in its technique. He did not participate, except very tentatively, with the two other leaders of the movement, Picasso and Braque, in their experiments with small many-faceted planes that derive from Cézanne. The cubist idiom somewhat obscured the space involvement but it greatly enhanced the rhythm, the abstract movement over and through the surface. Many of these more mannered works remain today among the finest examples of abstract art.[1]

---

[1] The geometrical styles evolved by Braque and Picasso were not difficult to imitate. Perhaps this is the reason for Cubism's sudden demise. Painters without the sensibility for rhythm and without a sense of architectural structure made an arid formula out of their idiom. So did advertising artists who by superficial adaptation gave the industry a new appeal.

Figure 25

Juan Gris, *Le Canigou*. Albright-
Knox Art Gallery, N. Y.

In Braque's painting *Valse* (Fig. 26), the multiple movements of planes and telescoping of spaces seem never-ending. Planes appear to shift as we look at them. Yet no complete image of anything can be discerned. It is an impression and at the same time an expression. It is not the kind of impression that Impressionists sought—not an impression of a world of light and atmosphere. It is an impression of movement. It is also an expression of sensations one experiences in shifting one's focus. This is the conceptual and poetic phase of the painting. From a formative point of view the work is a rhythmical and architectural construction in which measure—the relation of sizes—is the essence. (Note how the step motif and the distribution of dark accents carry out the oval shape of the composition.)

When we compare these cubist paintings of a generation ago with paintings of the last decade that employ cubist concepts of space we are impressed with the relative simplification of the latter. Not only is the technique broader and flatter, there is somewhat less involvement with small forms. Color has become less subservient to concept and more effective psychologically—that is, it elicits an immediate response, it affects one before assimilation of the form takes place.

To demonstrate the manner in which cubist ideas have been assimilated and simplified in present day art we reproduce two very different works. The *Still Life* (Fig. 27) by Giuseppe Ajmone possesses the interlocking planes of Gris in very simplified form. The illusion is of almost simultaneous flatness and depth (depending upon the shift of focus). Horizontal and vertical divisions of the surface flatten the composition in a Mondrian mode. But the spatial effects are very neatly attained. Recession is suggested by the diagonal edge of the table. A clear tension is expressed by the three juxtaposed patterns of light, dark, and middle values (curved and vertical stripes) on the upper left. The white cloth on which the grapes rest reaches over the table edge to become a white pattern on the wall, taking us from foreground to background. The design of all the curved forms taken together creates a flatness, an arabesque in a rigid architectural structure.

The second example is that of a post-cubist abstraction of interlocked space planes, *Le Globe de Mariage* (Fig. 28) by Jacques Villon. His color is lyrical, a delight to the eye. It is also functional in that it expresses the position and direction of the planes. In this forthright construction the planes intersect each other forming a complex of geometrical shapes, triangles and parallelograms, which provide, like the Braque, an almost

Figure 26

Georges Braque, *Valse*

73

Figure 27

Giuseppe Ajmone, *Still Life*. The
Collection of S. and I. Ullmann,
New York

Figure 28

Jacques Villon, *Le Globe de Mariage*
Courtesy Galerie Louis Carré, Paris

inexhaustible series of configurations. (Note, for example, the large square in the center of the composition and how each of its parts becomes a part of another form.) The use of a framework of horizontal and vertical patterns accomplishes precisely what the Lorenzetti painting, produced almost 600 years earlier does; it establishes a mood of serenity and order.

To sum up, the principle which unites early Renaissance religious painting, the 14th century view of an ancient city, a sophisticated cubist still life, and an abstraction of colored areas is that of a multiple or unfixed vision of space. The feeling we derive from contemplating such a space-relation is one of wonderment. It is the sense of wonder we experience when we are in a vast, imaginatively designed interior and our eyes take in simultaneously a complex of plane directions made by arches, columns, and walls. Architecture is capable of stimulating this space sensation. In a painting in which planes are organized into a spatial structure the form of such a structure resembles, in essence, architecture; for this reason it is termed architectonic. All of the examples given here belong to this category of architectonic space painting.

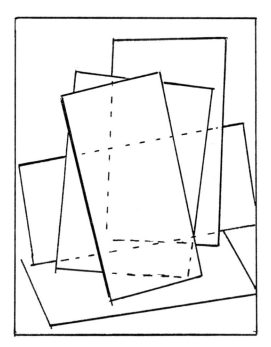

Diagram V-b

EXERCISES

The exercises outlined here are preliminary studies in charcoal. The painting of space compositions has been allocated to Chapter 9, *Twelve Painting Projects*, since that chapter follows the one on color usage. The notes on color will, it is believed, be helpful in the expression of the space-relation. Since our present concern is with the concept of architectonic space the structural form is the essence. This can be explored, at least in its basic aspects, in the medium of tonal charcoal drawing.

1. On charcoal paper 18″ x 24″, leaving a one-inch margin of white, put down an even gray tone. Hold the paper vertically. The space is almost entirely filled with four or five large rectangles placed at different axes and overlapping each other. All appear to be standing upon a large horizontal (but not entirely frontal) plane. Let some planes intersect others as if transparent. Diagram V-b is an example of the disposition of such planes. The procedure, once the space has been so divided, is to distribute values ranging from white to black in such manner that a flat surface design will result. This can be checked by turning the drawing upside down and studying it for balance. At the same time the relation of each plane to the one contiguous will be clearly stated spatially. The completed exercise should be sprayed with fixative and kept as a basis for a painting.

2. Holding the paper vertically, construct an interior of a room, ceiling, floor, a wall on each side, and a rear wall facing out, in other words the interior of a box. The side walls should vary in width and more space should be given to floor than to ceiling. On the wider side wall place a large vertical rectangle (as a mirror or picture), and a similar one on the rear wall. The first will thrust inward, the second will be frontal. Now place a table diagonally on the floor, showing the top surface, since we are looking down on this table. The table surface should be approximately the same size as the two rectangles on the walls. Each, however, has a different axis. Place a smaller rectangle on the table, as for example a magazine, one edge of which is continuous with one edge of the frontal rectangle. The space is now equivocal. In one view the magazine lying on the table in the near part of the room appears attached vertically to the mirror on the far wall. In another view the magazine is lying on the table. Try inventing other equivocal devices.

To complete the study, make one side wall black and distribute several other black patterns to attain a balance. With the kneaded eraser make all rectangles white. Introduce any other element to enhance the over-all pattern. Diagram V-c is a sketch of the idea.

3. The intersection of planes and the simultaneous appearance of frontal and inward-thrusting movement may be explored in charcoal as preparation for a non-objective painting. Pattern should be limited to rigid rectangles.

Our charcoal project, vertical once more, begins with a flat gray tone. On this an architectural form is constructed. It consists of many rectangles of varied sizes and values generally vertical and horizontal. But through the center of the area a series of vertical rectangles diminishing in length give the appearance of an inward-thrusting plane. Each of these rectangles seen individually is frontal and is part of the frontal design. But taken together they change their axes and turn inward. The frontal design is strengthened by a distribution of light and dark rectangles and the picture plane is further emphasized by an outlining of some of the rectangles to provide a linear pattern. Fig. 29 is an example of this exercise in architectonic space.

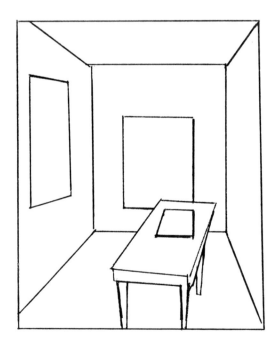

Diagram V-c

Figure 29

Grace Martin Taylor, *Composition of Receding Planes*. Courtesy of the artist

Part *II*

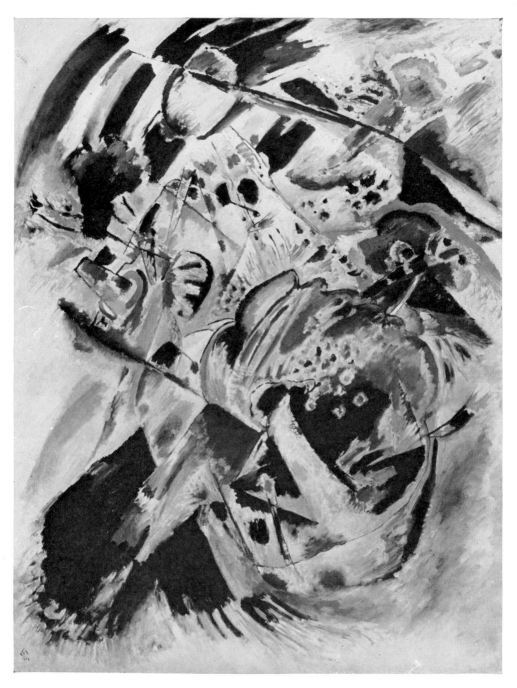

Figure 30

Vasily Kandinsky, *Painting: Winter,*
No. 868, 1914. The Solomon R.
Guggenheim Museum Collection

Fluid Space

6   The two basic tenets of Western paint-
ing composition since Giotto are, we have seen, the division
of the surface area and the illusion of depth. The depth is
at first, for the most part, three dimensional; with the advent
of cubist theory and the unearthing of certain early Italian
art the spatial illusion becomes equivocal—three-dimensional
space becomes relative, shifting with the focus of attention
and with the context. These two traditional aspects of
composition, surface division and space-relation are visible
in much of the new non-traditional, non-figurative painting
of the present. But other motivations and intentions have,
since the end of World War II, produced an art of painting
of a different form and image. The "new look" of much
contemporary painting reflects a new concept of the
function of painting and a new concept of space.

Before considering the change in intellectual attitudes
let us first describe in general the appearance of this
untraditional art. It is marked by a freedom of execution, an
apparent casualness, as if the painter were intent on saying

everything in one session or séance. The intimacy of the small canvas is rejected; in its place is a public statement of heroic dimensions, the intention of the painter apparently directed to museum display rather than to private taste. Novelty of surface is another aspect of the new art. And the spectator is aware of a subjective, self-analytic quality in the strange, seemingly private imagery or shapemaking of the artist.

The reasons for the change in the appearance of canvases in the past two decades are complex and diverse; they would take us into an analysis of sociological history, the new political awareness of a younger generation, the rise of psychoanalytic influences in art, and the intellectual acceptance of the faiths of Existentialism and Zen in place of the traditional philosophies. It may be said, in short, that the post-war generation rejected tradition in art as in every other category of living. (The same may be said of the Dadaists after World War I.)

What is significant in this rebellion is that it resulted in a change of painting idiom or style. Painters of an older generation, solidly trained in traditional art, have been strongly affected by this change. The spontaneity and vitality of expressionist art have been infectious even when coarseness and disorder have repelled. Competent formative painters have appropriated certain new techniques, have increased their format, and above all, have adopted a type of space organization which may be traced to early Chinese art, but which had been most effectively translated into Western painting by the Russian artist, Vasily Kandinsky.

The mode of space that Kandinsky employed is that of an unbounded area in which masses of cloud-like transparency and delicacy seem to pass over each other behind powerfully depicted symbols. A dynamic, almost explosive rhythm results. The symbols float, the space is open. Movement rather than structure is the essence of this form. For this reason the space concept is termed fluid. (See Fig. 30.)

While our interest is centered on this concept (to which we shall shortly return) it would be a serious omission to neglect mention of Kandinsky's friend and confrere who, from another direction, contributed almost as much to the development of the new image in painting. This was the Swiss painter, Paul Klee.

Klee was remarkably versatile; his styles and forms were more varied than Picasso's. He made use of every graphic mode whether ancient or modern. His draughtsmanship was delicate and expressive, his surrealistic imagery startlingly dramatic, his Freudian probing into the child mind remarkably astute. But from a purely painterly viewpoint his special gifts were his color relationships and rhythmic sense. Some of his finest works consist of simple rectangles of color in flat two-dimensional form, so harmoniously and rhythmically related that they recall musical orchestration and melody. In some of his odd compositions he retained a cubist style, but he made of them a tapestry of interlocking geometrical patterns rather than a serious expression of cubist space. Calligraphy and symbol mark most of his later works. It is these that impressed many young painters and deflected their interest from considerations of space-relation to an esthetic in which the evocative nature of symbols and shapes established the content. Form and content become one.

In his painting *Bal Champêtre* (Fig. 31) we see a forerunner of a school of contemporary art in which surface (or linear) rhythm, made of evocative symbols, is the content. But these symbols are not presented on a flat surface. Suggestion of a three-dimensional world is attained by variation of color and value in areas behind and around the symbols. Different values suggest different depths. These differences, however, are not sharply defined; they are as fluid as the spatial differences in some types of Chinese landscape painting. In paintings of this category we cannot with assurance say that this area is nearer or farther with relation to that; we *impute* positions to each colored surface according to the way we interpret the picture.

In the works of these two artists, Kandinsky and Klee, Existentialists, psychologists, Orientalists, and mystics found the inspiration if not the sources for their own development; so, likewise, did formative painters seeking new forms. Klee was the embodiment of the new spirit, the prober into the self, the detached, uninvolved analyzer of emotions. Vasily Kandinsky was the prophet of spirit against the material world—a spirit very colored by Chinese thought and art. For him the function of the painter was to produce works that were lyrical, that reflected, or rather projected the mystical and poetic spirit in man. This credo was expounded in his writings.[1]

Kandinsky came to this attitude after an experience with German Expressionism. He had painted romantic landscape in fauvist overstatement and distortion, gradually arriving at a powerful, rhythmic style. Then there occurred a sudden mystical revelation. Renunciation of all objective paint-

---

[1] It is most curious that both Klee and Kandinsky attempted to give a scientific basis to their art while professing a spiritual intention. Klee's mathematical equations are completely mystifying to mathematicians and Kandinsky's book *Point and Line to Plane* is a rigid formalization unworkable for students.

Figure 31

Paul Klee, *Bal Champêtre*. The Collection of Mr. and Mrs. Frederick Zimmermann, New York

ing, all romanticism, came one day when he walked into his studio, at dusk, and saw a few rays of departing light fall upon a canvas which had been turned upside down. He was enchanted by the effect, the mysterious world the painting in its accidental position evoked. He resolved to pursue painting for its imaginative and evocative values rather than as a commentary or report of the visible world. But he also enjoyed the sensuous aspect of color, the stimulus to his optic nerve and to his emotions. In his autobiography he says that the palette, after the painter has finished his day's work, is often more beautiful than any work of art. This statement would seem to imply that form was less important to him than the stimulus of colors; and that what he meant by "spiritual" was really only a sensuous enjoyment. But this, of course, was not the case. No European painting is more precisely ordered in its interval, the placing of symbols and motifs, and no painting is more evocative of mysterious spatial involvements than some of his non-figurative works. It is this latter quality of space-relation that is our particular concern.

Let us restate the nature of this space. A characteristic is the openness of the painting. The image it presents is of forms floating. There is no compact, tightly knit complex of color passages. In the open form the essence is the placing of significant motifs or descriptive elements, their relationship or interval. Behind these the spaces appear as layers, very delicately stated.

The concept of symbols floating in different planes or depths, the openness of the canvas, and the latitude permitted in the invention of shapes has appealed to imaginative painters because of the possibilities offered for expression of one's sense of rhythm, one's poetic fancy, and one's personal mode of putting together color. Release from both naturalistic illusion and acquired intellectual systems permits the painter to establish a mood through his own inventiveness, to evoke a feeling of wonderment and mystery. In discarding rigidity and intellectualization, painters of fluid space have turned to nature shapes, protoplasm, driftwood, bone and leaf shapes. Or, in many instances, they have used the most simple masses such as one might make by tearing paper. The accidental over-spillings, blots and blobs, added to the free shapes, enhance the effect of a mysterious world.

The application of paint, the technique, is also of major importance in paintings of fluid space. In some works, such as Afro's, the surfaces appear to be transparent, partially revealing fragments of line underneath the surface tone and so suggesting layers in depth. In other works the rich

Figure 32

José Guerrero, *Signs and Portents,*
1956. The Solomon R. Guggenheim
Museum Collection

variety of textures contributes to the painting's imaginative, mysterious nature. Subtlety in execution is essential. To attain delicate transitions from one area to the next, edges must be elusive. In losing and recovering edges, as in some Chinese landscape art, multiple layers of space, delicately expressed, are brought into a unity on the surface. The touch must be light and deft and appear to have been made easily and spontaneously. From such freedom of execution there emanates a lyrical grace, a verve that could not be attained by sharp contours, meticulous or showy technique, or plodding craft.

A few examples of open or fluid space will reveal the freedom of expression that marks this concept. José Guerrero's *Signs and Portents* (Fig. 32) would appear to be a collection of thoughtless smears were it not for the delicacy of nuance in the underlying tones. The dark patterns are in themselves somewhat monotonously placed, but in conjunction with the light patterns they establish a rhythm. It is apparent that the painter put down his symbols without any thought of revision or refinement. Uninhibited statement expressed with emotion appears to be his intention.

Giuseppe Santomaso is a Venetian painter of great sensitivity and refinement. In his *Composition* (Fig. 33), the pigment itself is so varied in textural quality that it adds greatly to the esthetic significance of the work. The half-tone reproduction, while depriving us of the pleasure and impact that fine color produces, reveals the subtlety of surface manipulation. The painting actually possesses very little content. Its essence is its form and the expressiveness of its execution. The space is composed of undefined depths, like clouds floating in the sky. The central mass of light establishes the stability. Fragments of line of different pressure and thickness, together with a few dark accents, keep our attention within the boundaries of the painting. There is a dynamic bursting outward from the center but the rhythm confines us to the area without barriers. The space is open.

A great many contemporary painters combine elements of one type of space with those of another. To be more exact, one is made subservient to the other. Painters who abstract from reality will sometimes permit their architecturally realized space planes to float out on the edges of the canvas, and conversely, painters working for an undefined, open space will resort to cubist tensions to strengthen their composition.

An example of such a combination is Fritz Winter's *Earthbound* (Fig. 34). Before analyzing the spatial tensions let us look at the work as a totality or unit. The spiraling knotted black line is nicely balanced by the three upright straight lines on the right. The circles are varied in size

Figure 33

Giuseppe Santomaso, *Composition*
The Collection of S. and I. Ullmann, New York

Figure 34

Fritz Winter, *Earthbound*, 1956
The Solomon R. Guggenheim
Museum Collection

91

and well placed. The broad bands of dark fill the surface area imaginatively and rhythmically. All appear to float. The surface, then, is extremely well designed. Now if we detach our interest from the whole and examine its parts we discover the spatial resources of the painter. Let us glance first at the two broad bands on the right. They form a kind of compressed parentheses holding the rectangular block (on poles) between them. The more curved band appears near, the longer one farther back. The block appears to thrust inward. Opposition of axis, the sandwiching of a light area between two darks, the thrust inward of a plane are all procedures used by architectonic space painters, notably Cubists. On the left side of the painting the calligraphy creates a flatness. The background, however, is not a flat tone. It is varied by a dark block at center-bottom and some dark above. But tension exists in the circular shapes. The lightest note appears nearest, the circle in the band on the left farther back, the large dark circle farthest. Now we no longer see the painting as a surface design. Each broad band is on a different spatial level, yet none is fixed. Thus in a context of fluid space the tensions of architectonic space are made effective.

Although different in style and image, the painting of Kenzo Okada, *Solstice* (Fig. 35), is a similar combination of modes of space. The flat design is detached from margins, the pattern placed in open areas. The dark rhythm is superbly achieved. But there are no mysterious layers of space, no undefined transitions expressed with sensuous or emotional verve. Instead there is a precision not only of execution but of placing; there is a weighing of quantities and a thoughtful ordering of shapes and spaces. If we look simultaneously at the black vertical shape in the foreground and at the equally dark square in the upper right, we experience a great separation in space that permits the entire diagonally placed center of the painting to lie between them. This is an elementary tension of darks.

It need hardly be said that the effectiveness of the type of painting described is dependent upon the sensibilities of the painter, particularly his sense of rhythm. The seemingly accidental elements in the canvas are made subservient to his feeling for order, movement, and balance. Perhaps it is too obvious or redundant to say that sensibilities are not to be confused with intellectualization; nevertheless, there must exist in the painter of sensibility an underlying concept—in this case the concept of a fluid space complex within which all the events of the painting take place.

The works reproduced in this chapter could not, we believe, have come into being without the examples of Klee's and Kandinsky's art. The rhyth-

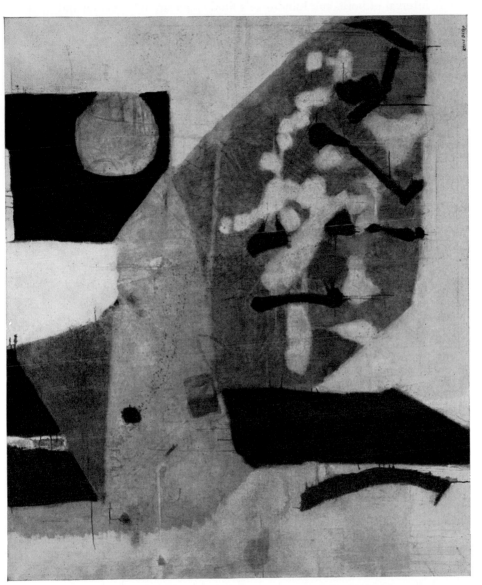

Figure 35

Kenzo Okada, *Solstice, 1954*
The Solomon R. Guggenheim
Museum Collection

mic interval of both, and Kandinsky's fluid space are interrelated and inter-
dependent. While the examples shown clarify the space concept, a more
detailed exposition of interval and rhythm will further elucidate this form.
This is the subject of the next chapter.

EXERCISES

As in the previous chapter the procedure will be to defer work in oil
to the section on Painting Projects. An introduction into the mode and
principle of fluid space, however, is possible through the medium of charcoal. Two preliminary exercises are given which may serve later as the
foundations for paintings.

1. First experiment with shapes. Make geometrical shapes somewhat
more complex than squares, circles, and triangles but not involved, complicated, or ornate. The shapes of old-fashioned door keys are a good
guide; they are composed of rectangles of various proportions. On a flat
gray ground distribute three or four shapes of black. The proper distribution is the essence of the exercise. An improper distribution is a static,
symmetrical, or even one. This may be avoided by heeding a few simple
strictures. Do not begin with a shape in the center of the area; nor in
any of the corners. Do not space shapes equidistant from each other. Do
not make the sizes of shapes similar. A good way of working is to think
in terms of diagonal relationship. For instance, if a large shape is placed
above and to the right of center, a smaller shape will be placed low and
to the left of center. A third shape will then be placed in a position where
it is nearer to one than to the other but of such weight or size as to
provide a balance. When this is satisfactory take the kneaded eraser and
establish three areas of light. Let one light juxtapose one black but keep
the two others independent. Here, too, the spacing should be uneven, not
only between the whites but between white and black. Actually this is an
exercise in interval and rhythm and belongs properly in the chapter that
follows. But it is given here to provide an experience in designing without
a prior division of the surface into pattern. The symbols should appear
to float in an open area.

2. The principle of this exercise is the making of space planes without
sharp definition. On a gray ground establish three cloud-like shapes only
a shade darker than the ground itself. The cloud-like shapes should have
their edges or contours smudged, or undefined. They should be varied in
size and, equally important, in spacing. But mainly they must each have

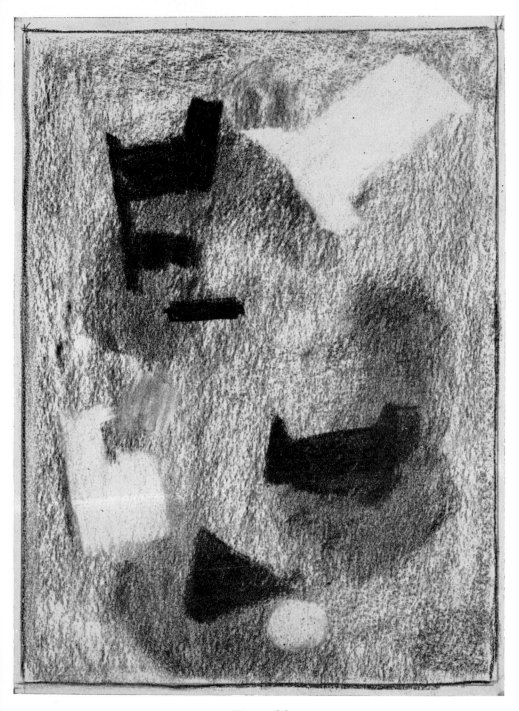

Figure 36

Morris Davidson, *Exercise in Fluid Space*

a different axis from the others. The slant of all, taken together, should present an elliptical movement. On top of these cloud shapes, or partly overlapping them, place shapes of dark and light similar to those in the previous exercise. In one or two instances overlap geometrical shapes with a simple rectangle, or a circle. Finally, vary the original gray ground of the base area by subtly modifying the tone. (See Fig. 36.)

The example shown is for the purpose of conveying some image of the exercise and is not to be regarded as a prototype or something to copy. The possibilities for variety are endless. The crucial step in the composition is the first one, namely, the making of the indeterminate shapes. Note in the example the manner in which these masses are tipped to relate to each other.

These two exercises will serve as schematic introductions to a form of non-figurative painting more and more widely practiced. While they may not be very effective without color, they will indicate the nature of the organization of a painting of fluid space.

Interval
and Rhythm

7   If we turn back to Fig. 11 (p. 20) in
the first chapter, de Stael's *Composition on a White Ground,*
we now, in the light of the exposition in the preceding
chapter, see it in a fresh way. Instead of looking for the
division of surface area we see it as groupings of dark
spots that appear to float over the surface, and possibly in
depth. What gives this seemingly casual painting interest is
the variety in the sizes and clusters, and the spaces
between. It is interesting to see this dark pattern expressed
as light. In reversing the values as in the negative (Fig. 37)
we experience the feeling of looking at an entirely different
picture. The design of the spots is the same, only the
psychological reaction, the mood, is different. In both we are
intrigued by quantities and spacing.

Let us compare these two reproductions with a
photograph of an African rock painting (Fig. 38). Here is
a herd of cattle drawn in primitive fashion without regard to
perspective. The picture fascinates us by its arrangement
of the animals and even more by the inventiveness and

Figure 37

Negative of de Stael's painting,
Figure 11.

Figure 38

African Rock Painting
Courtesy La Guilde du Livre

Diagram VII-a

variety of shapes. Two or three cows are dark silhouettes but the others are depicted in black and white patterns so that an abstract element, imaginative shape, transmutes this primitive expression into an esthetic object; it is not a mere description. The spacing between the imaginative shapes, the clusters and separations, provide us with a remarkable demonstration of the art of interval.

The word *interval* is defined in the dictionary as a "space of time between two points or events." In painter's language this definition may be shortened slightly by the elimination of the two words, "of time." The

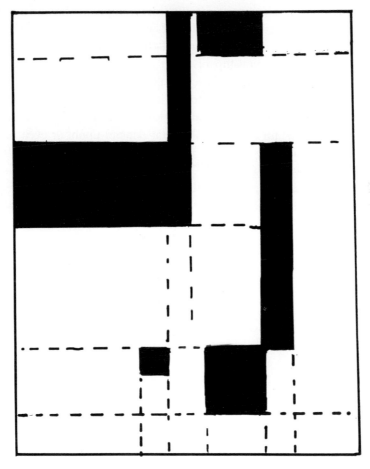

Diagram VII-b

"events" in an abstract or non-objective painting are the arresting notes of color, the shapes or symbols, or any imaginative configurations. The spaces between such effective notes are the intervals. Intervals may be monotonously repetitious or they may be imaginatively varied and rhythmical. Rhythmical interval is an essential, indeed a basic element of painting composition, particularly where the space concept is fluid.

The phrase just used—"a basic element of composition"—appeared in the first chapter when we spoke of the division of the surface area. We may regard such division as one basic principle, and rhythmic interval as another, but in actuality both elements are sometimes complementary parts of the same principle. This can be made clear if we look at the Diagrams VII-a and VII-b. By isolating the spaces around the effective notes (in this case shapes), we see the relationship of space division to interval. The space is negative, the shapes in their intervals positive.

It should be stated here that interval is not the only means of attaining rhythm in the painting. A composition constructed by well defined planes moving in certain directions does not depend upon, or even require, symbols or other effective notes for rhythm. Such, for example, is Villon's abstraction in Chapter 5 (Fig. 28). The tensions of the planes themselves provide the rhythm. But where spatial differences are barely defined and the surfaces delicately modulated, whatever is strongly stated will assume great importance. The problem is to place these strong notes, symbols, or pattern in such manner that no single one will hold our attention. On the contrary, every one should suggest a visual leap to the next. This can only be achieved by variety in the sizes of the notes, their shapes and axes and, particularly, in the spacing of them. When these requirements are met, the movement through the area is esthetically exciting. We say of such work that it is "musical."

Painting of this order, it must be repeated, is the product of a developed sensibility and cannot be achieved by mental calculation. While our diagram shows that a division of the negative space is implicit in the positioning of the intervals of "events," of effective notes, it is not to be assumed that calculated division of the surface will itself yield a rhythmic movement. This is precisely the error of such mathematical "sure-fire" formulas as "dynamic symmetry," "the golden section," etc. There is no doubt that prolonged experience in making arresting divisions of the surface will develop in the painter a consciousness of non-symmetrical balance and an awareness of variety in sizes and shapes. When a symbol is placed in relation to another, consciousness of the intervening space must be automatic. One can, by dint of perseverance, develop a keen feeling for rhythm; but one cannot achieve it by calculation, because the weight, size, pressure, and intensity of each note demand a reciprocal statement. Calculation or mathematical process cannot take such variables into account.

The art of the East is notable for its interval. Let us therefore look at two examples of Japanese interval. Since there are no halftones to complicate relationships the black will stand out sharply. The Japanese print of reeds, attributed to Hokusai (Fig. 39), is a clear example of calligraphy,

Figure 39

Hokusai, *Reeds*

and of spots so placed in the area that one's attention is led from point to point within it. The making of the original was undoubtedly a spontaneous succession of brush strokes. The Japanese artist strives for decisiveness, deftness, and variability in expression. Unhesitating statement communicates a lightness of spirit to the spectator. But this illusion of swift abandon is achieved only by prolonged and rigorous practice. If we were coldly to analyze the negative space we would discover an inventive division of the surface. The artist no doubt would have been repelled by such an analysis, insisting that every gesture was dictated only by his feeling—as it assuredly was. Nevertheless, the rhythm relates to the total area, to the negative space as well as to the "events."

Often the painter combines the rhythmic interval of dark pattern with a clearly stated division of the area. From this combination a classical composition results—classical in that a sense of measure is retained throughout even while our glance is momentarily focused on the surface rhythm. We have seen an excellent example of this in the Japanese print reproduced in the first chapter, *Three Maidens* (Fig. 4), by Shigenobu.[1]

The mode of expression in each of these Japanese prints is different: in one the distribution of designed shapes in the area enhances the rhythm; in the other a configuration of lines and spots of great variety, not only in the weight and pressure of the stroke but in the play of opposing directions, creates the rhythm. Both usages have been adopted by contemporary painters, as we shall see. The obvious differences in style between contemporary expression and classical Japanese art may, however, be attributed to dissimilar objectives in the matter of performance. The Japanese artist strives to be rhythmically expressive *but within a convention*; the Western artist prefers to be as unhampered by tradition as possible. Thus, while making use of age-old principles, the non-figurative painter of today pushes aside all barriers to theme and style.

A painter whose influence upon a younger generation has been great, particularly in Germany and in the United States, was the late German artist Willi Baumeister. Because of his avant-garde ideas as painter and teacher he was discharged from his post as professor of painting at the Frankfort Academy by the Hitler regime and forbidden to paint. But he

---

[1] Among the most notable exponents of this combination of flat plane and rhythmic interval are the Persian miniaturists. Their art is a never ending delight in its fusion of descriptive fantasy and rhythmic interval. A good collection of color reproductions of Persian and Hindu miniatures provides an excellent study for the abstract painter.

Figure 40

Willi Baumeister, *Metamorphosis
1951*. Courtesy of Mrs. Willi
Baumeister

Figure 41

Willi Baumeister, *Fra Diavolo 1951*
Courtesy of Mrs. Willi Baumeister

continued to produce novel and arresting non-objective paintings in secrecy in the town of Stuttgart. After the defeat of the Nazis he was appointed professor at the Art Academy in Stuttgart where his inspiring teaching was instrumental in changing the course of German non-figurative painting.

Baumeister disdained the conventional and even the agreeable in art. But if it is possible to make an arresting esthetic unity out of unappealing and sometimes repulsive elements this imaginative artist succeeded in doing so. On the other hand he occasionally achieved magnificent color organizations that captivate the most discriminating eye. In all his compositions, those that enchant and those whose imagery repels, there is an imaginative power that is given to few artists. The shapes he employed seemed derived either from organic material, protoplasm, insect life, bone forms, and rotted leaves; or from archaic art of the Near East. He was one of the first non-objective painters to construct "ideograms," evocative shapes patterned on the ancient art of the Sumerians. But his major attachment was to nature—the shapes of observable phenomena. Here we reproduce two of his paintings, *Metamorphosis* (Fig. 40), which seems to express the coagulating movements of cells under a microscope, and *Fra Diavolo* (Fig. 41), a symbolic evocation of the legendary bandit-monk.

In Baumeister's paintings the weight and position, the space intervals, the use of light shapes as well as dark, create the rhythm in a most original style. Yet however original the style, the concept (of a rhythmic movement attained by imaginatively distributed spots of black and white) is older than history. Compare Baumeister's *Metamorphosis* with the African Rock Painting (p. 99).

While the shapes in *Fra Diavolo* seem carefully weighed and placed, those in *Metamorphosis* suggest an element of accident. This was touched on in the description of Kandinsky's art. At the risk of being redundant a significant point must be stressed.

If we drop a few blobs of ink on a surface, the accidental variation in size, shape, and position may delight or even fascinate us. We could not contrive such diversity by planning. Nor could the effect be visualized beforehand. But as we look at this configuration with reference to the area in which it occurs we note that it bears no special relation to the boundaries. It may occupy too small a part, may "weight down" one corner, or be too centered. The resourceful artist, possessing a sense of rhythm, will not be content to multiply the accidental spottings and effects but will proceed to give a structural meaning to the original accident by

adding whatever is necessary to the unity of the work. He will make the
accidental rhythmical.[2]

From Baumeister's shapes to Jackson Pollock's scribbles and shapeless
blobs was an inevitable step. The "look" of the modern painting was
transformed by the introduction of shapelessness. The impulsive automatic
and accidental appearance provided the new note. This became the talis-
man of much abstract painting, even of that style which is not "action
painting," not feverishly cluttered by uninhibited energy, but which, on the
contrary, is relatively calm. Consider, for example, the painting by Corpora
(Fig. 42), a contemporary Italian painter. Here we see amorphous forms,
stretched like a stringy and sticky substance and floating in a steamy void.
At first glance the shapeless masses appear accidentally dropped on the
canvas. But there is rhythm here. The masses, spots, and scratchings fall
into an order. And although we miss the delight of the luminous blue
color of the original we respond to the sensitive rhythm that evokes the
lyrical feeling of Chinese art.

Not all interval in contemporary painting, however, is expressed in the
style of seemingly accidental or shapeless passages. The English abstractionist Ben Nicholson, working in a rigid geometrical style, achieves a
notable rhythm of interval. So, likewise, does the Italian painter Franco
Gentilini. The latter's painting, *Figure and Table* (Fig. 43), is a fine
example of distribution of dark pattern in a tightly controlled organization.

The examples so far shown have been restricted to the rhythmic function
of dark pattern. In compositions of a dark tonality—low-keyed paintings—
the pattern of light functions similarly (as we have seen in the negative
of de Stael's painting). Color may itself create the rhythm without the
aid of strong values; this is the subject of the next chapter. But there is
another element, line, which can provide the spirited movement, the *élan*,
to the painting.

Linear rhythm is one of the most difficult elements of composition to
acquire. It comes naturally to some painters while others must struggle
to attain it by constant experiment and search for a formula. In current
practice it takes many forms; sometimes it is a flowing continuity, sometimes a configuration of small fragments, sometimes a writing or scribbling.

---

[2] If the work of Jackson Pollock stands out from that of most of his imitators
it is not because he induced better accidental effects but because he was able
to subordinate such effects to a larger unity—by sublimating them to a fluid surface in
which the placing of major accents dominated the total area.

Figure 42

Antonio Corpora, *Pittura 1958*
Courtesy of Galleria Pagliani, Rome

Figure 43

Franco Gentilini, *Figure and Table*
Courtesy of Galleria D'Arte del
Naviglio, Milan

The line pattern of the Florentine school of the Renaissance has been admired and analyzed by many writers. It is perhaps an oversimplification to say that the characteristic attribute of this line is its graceful and flowing continuity—that is to say, the contours of figures and robes are not confined to what they describe but are connected with each other so that the spectator's interest is carried through the total area by these contours, independent of their descriptive function. Such use of line, then, becomes an esthetic attribute, an abstraction. Centuries later Gauguin revives Botticelli's method and many post-impressionist painters follow his lead. The restoration of rhythmical line as an esthetic attribute of painting appears to have been a reaction to the complete disregard of line by the Impressionists.

In our reference to Cubism in Chapter 5, in which the spatial interplay of small facets was discussed, we wrote of the "abstract" character of interlocking configurations and showed a reproduction of a typical work, *Valse* (Fig. 26, p. 73) by Braque. If we turn back to this work and view it as surface, we become aware of the complex interplay of line fragments, of curve and angle. This use of line not only sharpens the image of each small form, it constitutes a pattern in itself, it is an abstract linear rhythm. This is an element of cubist art retained by some non-figurative painters who otherwise have no interest in cubist concept or form.

Another influence upon the development of line as a rhythmic element in the painting was the discovery of the esthetic character of unintelligible writing—a page of Persian manuscript, a Chinese inscription, a Japanese calligraphic screen, Egyptian hieroglyphs, etc. Many abstract painters derive ideas of line pattern from such unreadable, but esthetically moving configurations. Others, more psychologically oriented, find in the impulsive, and even compulsive, scribblings of children, patterns of line which, when incorporated into a sophisticated painting form, provide a startling freshness. Such drawing of children may be divided roughly into two categories: the naïve, relaxed delineation of objects in a continuous or interlocking pattern (such as Paul Klee's imitations of child vision), and, at the other extreme, violent, chaotic scrawls (which we may see all about us).

With this brief introduction to contemporary uses of line let us look at a few examples taken from modern European art.

GINO SEVERINI

Fig 44: A gouache in free calligraphic style. The line, besides being rhythmical on the surface, suggests thrusting planes—a concept deriving from Cubism. Note the variation in the weight or pressure of various lines. The black symbols oppose the heavy diagonal line dividing the area.

Figure 44

Gino Severini, *Gouache N. 82*
Courtesy of Brera Gallery, Milan

GERHARD FIETZ

Fig. 45, Forms and Lines: Also cubist in its spatial concept, this work is, however, free of cubist style. It is a calligraphic play of "hard" lines against "soft" tones. Planes of space are clearly separated but the strong tensions and distribution of circle motifs unite the composition in a forceful—if less obvious—rhythm than the Severini.

Figure 45

Gerhard Fietz, *Forms and Lines*
From *Abstrakte Maler Lehren*
(Verlag Heinrich Ellermann,
Munich)

ZAO WOU-KI

Fig. 46, The Hunter: As dynamic and Western as is Severini's line, so mysteriously quiet and Eastern is this calligraphy of the Parisian Chinese abstractionist. The varied configurations that are here assembled may have symbolic meaning for the artist—a few, like the tiny hunter in the lower center and the animal in the upper right, may be identifiable—but it is the rhythm that gives esthetic meaning to this work. Note, for example, the line pattern of exquisite sensitivity in the lower left corner.

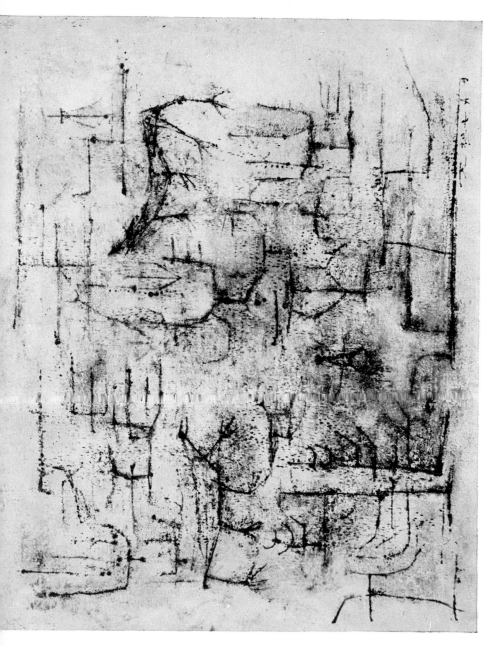

Figure 46

Zao Wou-ki, *The Hunter*. The
Collection of S. and I. Ullmann,
New York

ROLF CAVAEL

Fig. 47, Abstract Painting: *This is the late expression of one of Germany's most disciplined modern painters. It is his effort to free himself from his knowledge and experience and to recapture the spontaneous, almost compulsive expression of the uninhibited child mind. What results inevitably from such intention is a work that may resemble the idiom of the child but which, in its sensitive and cultivated feeling for rhythmic interval, presents an image of extreme sophistication.*

Figure 47

Rolf Cavael, *Abstract Painting*. The
Collection of S. and I. Ullmann,
New York

119

Fig. 48: In this Composition No. 129 the artist makes both fusion and counterpoint of line and tone. The impression is of Chinese characters freely interpreted and held together by sweeping and graceful arabesques. The small dark squares at the ends of the lines are rhythmically distributed, as are the light spots. Concept and style share the contemporary feeling of being uninvolved and direct. This avoidance of complexity is most readily felt when we look at the following painting by that pioneer of non-objective art,

Vasily Kandinsky.

HANS THIEMANN

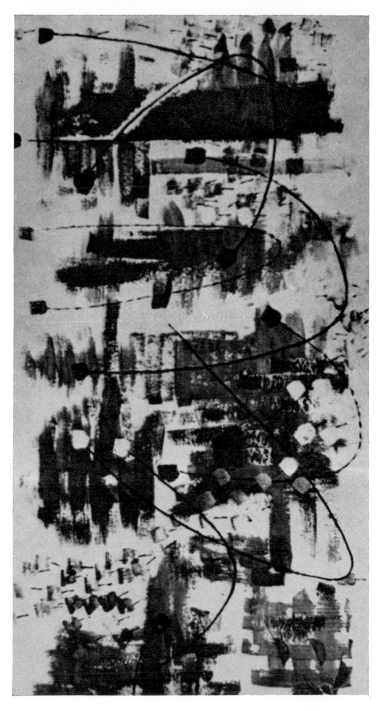

Figure 48

Hans Thiemann, *Composition No.
129.* From *Abstrakte Maler Lehren*
(Verlag Heinrich Ellermann,
Munich)

VASILY KANDINSKY

Fig. 49, Black Lines No. 189: It is most fitting to show here the work of a pioneer in abstract line rhythm. Painted in 1913, all of the freedom of contemporary expression is here anticipated. The playful and impulsive line seen against contradictory movements imparts an excitement that is as strongly felt today, when we are accustomed to violent painting, as it was half a century ago. Not only is there a tremendous variety, an unlimited imaginative resourcefulness, in quality of line, but its disposition with regard to the light and dark spotting adds to the over-all rhythm.

Figure 49

Vasily Kandinsky, *Black Lines*, 1913
The Solomon R. Guggenheim
Museum Collection

EXERCISES IN INTERVAL

1. Arrange a small still life group of five or six objects against a background of divided areas—areas which vary in size and shape. The table surface, too, should comprise several varied shapes. Make a clean line drawing (as in Chapter 3) stressing rhythmic movement. In this drawing place patterns of nearly solid black, distributing them for varied interval, size, and shape. Use no gray tones and no shading or gradations. The blacks will be an arbitrary design, not a faithful copy of the dark places visible in the set-up, but perhaps suggested by the set-up. Diagram VII-c shows the nature of such a drawing.

When the drawing appears to be satisfactory in its space division and balance, it may be transferred (with variations) on to canvas or board for painting. Wash in the dark areas with diluted black. Then, either adhering to the colors of the set-up or inventing an entirely different pal-

Diagram VII-c

ette, complete the stain. When the stain is dry, paint for variation in surface texture, allowing some of the stained areas to remain.

2. In this exercise the same set-up is the basis for a more imaginative and inventive design of dark pattern. Instead of making the images of the objects explicit, the intention is to use them as points of departure for a more integrated rhythm. (See Diagram VII-d.) Paint this version in imagined (unrealistic) color.

3. A useful experience in interval is the making of a collage. Cut out some simple (not ornate) shapes of black construction paper. Avoid static or symmetrical shapes such as perfect squares or T and Y shapes. Vary the sizes, making one black dominant. Paste up areas of pale yellows and off-white. Distribute six or seven black shapes in varied interval. Then add one note or pattern of brilliant yellow.

Although dramatic and imaginative interval is a most vital requisite of non-figurative painting, no exercise in the making of a large composition

Diagram VII-d

is given here. This is because such a composition involves a coordination of interval, linear rhythm, and color. Color is the subject of the next chapter. The painting projects following that chapter will afford an opportunity to create a rhythmical non-figurative painting. Here it is pertinent and timely to begin an experience with line as an esthetic element independent of its descriptive function.

EXERCISES IN LINE RHYTHM

1. To develop an interest in line independent of its descriptive function, that is, as an esthetic end in itself, a practical method is to learn to see it as a material substance. To do this get a batch or coil of baling wire in the hardware store. With wire-cutting pliers cut this wire into various lengths from three inches to a foot. Make some perfectly straight, curve others, and bend some into various shapes. Take a handful of such an assortment (at least a dozen) and holding them about eighteen inches above a white surface 20" x 24", let them drop. The accidental configurations will surprise and often delight you. Repeat this experiment in "accidental esthetics" many times. You will find yourself moving several of the wires to achieve a better balance or to open up a congested area. When you are impelled to do this you have arrived at an appreciation of line as an element independent of its function of delineating nature.

2. Cover charcoal paper with a solid gray tone. Without permitting any sharp edges, lightly erase some of the tone and darken other areas. Using soft vine charcoal draw freely over the surface. Vary the lines from thin to thick. Scribble in some areas and draw with precision in others.

There is, of course, a difference between handling charcoal and controlling the brush. Many students who handle charcoal ably find it difficult to make expressive line with a brush. A good way of gaining experience is to use old discarded boards or canvases as a background for line making. Use a No. 2 long flat bristle brush. Dilute black pigment with a drop of turpentine. Hold the brush-end lightly between thumb and forefinger. Begin by making long straight lines. Poise the brush at the upper end of the projected line and pull downward gently. Try various thicknesses of line. Once a variety of expression is attained, curved and wavy lines may be attempted. The essential is to hold the brush at the tip end and to use the arm, not the fingers, to make the line.

When some quality is achieved it will be fruitful to interpret the charcoal exercise in paint, selecting any one color for an over-all tonality.

The rhythm of interval and the rhythm of line are the skeletal structure of the painting. But color is its heart, its breath of life. No system can impart the magic of color but much can be said about its properties, its function, and its misuse. Color, like shape, undergoes changes in fashion and usage. While, therefore, no one can pretend to make a colorist out of a painter by admonitions and formulas, the individual already endowed with a color-sense may benefit by a clarification of its properties and modes. These are the subject of the next chapter.

Exploring
Color

8   If form is the attribute that makes
abstract art intelligible and deserving of attention (and
that lifts representational work out of the category of mere
illustration), color is the element that may induce delight
and that should imbue the painting with the unique psyche
and spirit of the artist.

Periodically color systems are disseminated purporting to
give the painter a method for achieving satisfactory, if not
foolproof, harmonies and relationships of color. These
are seized upon as revelations not only by professional
painters but by their enthusiastic confreres in school and
college art faculties—but only temporarily, until a new
system appears. Seeing how readily one system supersedes
another, one must conclude that all doctrinal systems are
attempting to do the impossible. They propose to contain
art in a formula as Ulysses' bags contained the winds. Yet they
are all of them not without some use; they have the merit
of arousing the painter's curiosity, causing him to explore
his palette in new ways. Any experience with the palette may

be fruitful, possibly yielding surprises and discoveries. After half a century of painting a painter concludes that the possibilities of color are infinite.

Nevertheless, there is information one may pass on which has the virtue of preventing vapid, banal, strident, or just muddy color. There are usages suited to some purposes and not to others. These merit discussion. Color may create naturalistic illusions; but it may also intensify certain aspects of appearance or even of truths underlying appearance. In the latter instance the color is termed functional (as distinct from mimetic), since it is employed as a language to convey ideas—ideas about physical phenomena, recession, value, and the space-relation. Functional color, as is generally known, is the great contribution to painting of Cézanne. Whereas Impressionist color had concerned itself with light and vibration, and later with delicate, often sentimental effects, Cézanne evolved a language of color to express structure and space.

Color may also induce psychological states. The late, noted mystic, Nicholas Roerich, in a syllabus on painting, once listed the psychological properties of hues. Blue, for example, is the celestial color that induces serenity and contemplation, etc. We are all familiar with the slaughtered animals of Soutine, the gory innards that fascinate and revolt simultaneously. And at the other extreme the sanitary, prissy coloration of Marie Laurencin, a perverse, sophisticated (and spurious) puritanism. In non-figurative painting, where the viewer may make his own association of color with theme, the psychological importance of tonality is obvious.

The modes of these various usages can, of course, be learned. One may also benefit from technical information—the knowledge of new pigments and media which extend the range of color beyond that of an orthodox palette.[1] To this aspect of the subject we shall return shortly.

To discourse on color at all it is necessary to establish a lexicon of terms. The color as named, red, violet, brown, etc., is the *hue*. The color seen through narrowed eyes, the painter's squint that filters out most of the hue, is the *color value*. (*Value* is the degree of light and dark.) *Tone* is a general term to express a passage of painting—it is hue plus value; but other subtle factors enter into the definition, for example, *density* and *luminosity*, or even the textural quality. *Density* is the opaqueness, the

---

[1] A simple permanent palette for beginners is composed of Alizarin Crimson, red, orange and yellow cadmiums, Zinc Yellow, Titanium White, Cobalt and Ultramarine Blue, Viridian Green, and Ivory Black. For a full discussion of the uses of this basic, prismatic palette see the author's book *Painting for Pleasure* (Hale, Cushman & Flint, 1938).

thick buttery quality of the pigment. Some pigments such as the cadmiums are naturally heavy and dense. *Luminosity* is the glow of the color as seen in stained glass or when a dark bottle is held up to the light. (Viridian and Alizarin possess this property when applied thinly.) The term "brightness" should be abolished because it is inexact since it confuses light with intensity; in its place the word *intensity* should be used. Intensity refers to the color, its purity undiluted with light or white. (Although some very dark pigments such as Ultramarine Blue are most intense when a very small amount of white is added.) *Tonality* is not to be confused with tone. It refers to the over-all dominant coloration of the canvas. High and low key describe the *value* (degree of light) of the tonality.

Prismatic color refers to the primary and secondary colors of the prism: red, yellow, blue, violet, orange, and green. Pastel colors are prismatic colors loaded or diluted with white. Earth colors are dense and in hue are not primary or secondary but tertiary; that is, in order to match them more than two primary hues are required. Since some pigments are heavy and fatty, others thin and transparent, it is important to know how to make use of the distinctive character of each. Such knowledge may be acquired by periodic experiment on a white glass or similar palette (white "marlite," a coated masonite, is excellent), putting together dense and luminous tones.

Pastel color may be said to derive from Impressionist painting, following the discovery of the prism. It is sweet and pretty and has become banal; it is generally avoided by contemporary abstract painters. Overly rich, deep, luminous, "stained glass" colors tend to be romantic (in the sense of Rachmaninoff's chords). Strident color is generally an unrelieved use of saturated prismatic color—like flags. The conclusion which may be drawn from these classifications is that a painting done in an exclusive bracket or category of color is apt to be unexciting. Inventive, imaginative, vital color results from the putting together of tones from various color groups (just as a vital dynamic community is one made up of persons of various and diverse ethnic groups).

While much strident color has been in evidence in recent years, partly as a result of the impact upon painting of German and American Expressionists, there has also been a noticeable development in the flexibility and range of color. This is attributable partly to new techniques and also to the creation of new pigments through chemistry, as mentioned before. The pthalocyanine colors blue and green, usually labeled by the name of the manufacturer, as for example, Johnson Blue, have taken the place of fugitive, murky Prussian Blue, and of weak Viridian, respectively. And the appearance of a variety of cool reds and violets of quinacridone pigment (also labeled by manufacturer's name) has stimulated painters to evolve, in conjunction with subdued tones, new and more vivid harmonies. Another comparatively recent addition to the painter's resources in attaining clean and glowing color is acrylic pigment (pigment ground in an acrylic medium, and commonly called plastic paint), very quick-drying and brilliant. The white is particularly useful for underpainting; it is also serviceable for restoring the fresh surface of the canvas after an area has been scraped off as unsatisfactory. Several of the large color makers are now offering various acrylic "gels" to be mixed with pigment in place of a varnish or siccatif medium. This substance keeps the color glowing as originally applied, preventing the "sinking-in" or oxidation of the color and consequent dead spots on the canvas.

The new look in contemporary painting may also be attributed to the current practice of avoiding artists' brushes. Practically all abstract painters use hardware store brushes and kitchen spatulas, in addition to their regular equipment, to apply the pigment.

So much for the technical tid-bits. It must be borne in mind that no technical innovations or accessories will take the place of good working methods. The mottos which should be hung in every school studio are (1) *Scrape frequently*; (2) *Paint slowly but make the canvas appear as if it were executed in one session.* To assure the second, one must rigorously observe the first.

The exercises which follow are not elementary. They are intended to widen the experience of painters already capable of mixing desired tones without struggle, and already proficient in applying paint. They have been devised for two reasons. In the first place there are many competent students in a rut as far as their use of color is concerned. Habit has overcome imagination and invention—has imprisoned them in a formula. In the second place many painters regard color as a technique belonging to their type of painting, as a flag represents a country. The really creative painter regards color very differently; it is a language of expression. As stated earlier, it may be used functionally to express volume and recession as Cézanne used it. It may be spatial as in Braque and Gris, lyrical and evocative as in Kandinsky. It may be airy, mysterious, dramatic, startlingly pure. It is sometimes exquisitely decorative but it also has the capacity to stir one's deepest feelings. Because of the unlimited capacity of color to express sensations as a language expresses ideas, it is reasonable to hold that the painter should explore the *uses* of the language of color just as a writer, learning his profession, explores the uses of language.

For the painting student with little experience other than reproducing the colors of objects set before him, some preliminary steps are advisable. The first experience with color in an abstract sense may be had by setting out eight or nine prismatic colors plus white and black on a large smooth white surface (glass, or "marlite" as mentioned previously) and then making units or complexes of color in the following manner: Using the knife put down a block of dense gray (black and white). Leave white space and put down a note of pearly gray made of white, Alizarin, and Viridian. Near these put down a dense brown (Cadmium Red and Ivory Black) and a luminous brown (Alizarin, Ultramarine Blue, and orange). In the intervening white spaces, using small brushes, paint pure colors such as yellow-green, rose-red, or yellow-orange, filling out the pattern. Now paint a light flesh color outside the first dense gray and a passage of pure black outside the brown. Next to the black put a stripe of light pink. This unit will comprise neutral, pastel, prismatic, luminous, and dense color.

Another unit might consist of a collection of tones of tan, like sand, Manila paper, and raw wood. In intervening spaces paint pure Cobalt Blue and Viridian. Juxtapose black.

Make other units of your own, keeping in mind the objective of combining colors of different categories or families.

EXERCISES

The first exercise is intended to provide practice in applying paint freely. On a canvas or board held vertically, and using a two-inch house-painting brush, cover a surface with various tones of gray. Vary the direction of strokes (which should be made with the flat plane of the brush, not with the side edges). When the surface area has been covered, not too heavily, lay aside the brush and in its place use a flexible kitchen spatula. With this pick up some combination of vivid color without mixing it too thoroughly on the palette. This batch of color should be generous. Apply it heavily with a slightly slanting stroke. Do not work over or rub in the pigment, but leave the edges ragged where they are so. Then wipe the spatula. Mix a complementary batch of vivid color and apply it at a slightly different slant and in a different size from the first passage. Limit the colors to three, but paint six or seven passages in similar fashion with variations of the three colors.

The purpose of this effort is to experience a freedom in paint application. It is an antidote to tightness, timidity, and tickling of the surface. It may even have esthetic merit in its spontaneity and freshness.

2. This exercise has as its objective the development of sensitivity to nuances of color. It will also provide some experience with a few of the newer pigments. The exercise is, in a sense, in triplicate; that is to say it involves three canvases, red, yellow, and blue. Each canvas is to be composed of freely painted blocks (rectangles without sharp edges) of variations of one hue. A glance at the three lists below will indicate the many possibilities for such variations. The blocks should of course be varied in size and proportion to avoid a checkerboard effect.

When the color in various nuances, not only of hue but of value, has covered the canvas, small notes of any complementary or entirely different color may be distributed to enliven the surface. A few of the edges may be darkly outlined to provide a rhythm, but this is optional. The list of pigments given here is offered as a suggestion and may be supplemented by other related pigments. (Q is the symbol for quinacridone, Pth for pthalocyanine.)

Red	Yellow	Blue
Q Red	Naples	Cerulean
Q Rose Red	Cadmium Pale	Cobalt
Alizarin Crimson	Cadmium Medium	Ultramarine
Cadmium Red Light	Cadmium Deep	Pth Blue
Q Violet	Raw Sienna	Indigo

Figure 50 is an example of this exercise in the blue version.

Figure 50

Morris Davidson, *Blue Painting*

Twelve
Painting Projects

9 The eight preceding chapters constitute
a preparation for this working section. They form an
esthetic basis without which the projects might be simply
distorted into games. The exercises will be best achieved
when supervised or at least evaluated by a professional painter
or teacher. But even without a teacher, if the student has
first conscientiously done the preliminary charcoal
studies in more than one version, he will have experienced the
act of creative painting. Providing such experience is the
raison d'être of this book.

The projects are arranged in a progressive order; they move
from the representational to the semi-abstract and then to
the non-figurative. Even if the painter prefers to remain
in the semi-abstract category it will be useful to explore the
forms that are to him less appealing. All painting is most
effective when performed with assurance. It is only by
understanding the principles and concepts pertinent to a
particular form—an understanding derived from experience
—that the painter may avoid confusion or inconsistency

in his work. Consistency is more than a jewel in the art of painting, it is its very life. The wider one's experience, the more selective of formal elements will one be in his work. Consistency develops out of selectivity, and authenticity and vitality are the result.

PROJECTS IN PLAUSIBLE AND ARCHITECTONIC SPACE

1. The painting of the easel theme described in Chapter 1 is much less difficult than the drawing. The color will be gray, in various nuances, except for the canvases which will be various tones of white, warm and cool, and the brown easels. When this composition of a restrained tonality is near completion several more vivid notes may be circulated. These may be in some instances on the off-white canvases, as designs, or on the rear wall, or even on the floor. The interval of these more vivid notes is important for the rhythm and should not, therefore, be haphazard.

The dark lines of the easels will create a linear movement through the painting. This may be enhanced by stressing some of the horizontal edges of the canvas.

A further aid to the composition will be the turning of one of the easels in the foreground to thrust inward, slanting its base and making the canvas on it converge toward the rear wall.

While this painting involves the division of the surface area in an imaginative fashion, it also is concerned with space-relation in limited depth. For this reason the floor should not be too deep and recessive. Nor should the canvases in the rear, or the rear wall itself, be weakly painted.

2. In Chapter 2 the diagrams II-c and II-d show the difference between distance and the space-relation. The exercise here deals with expressing the space-relation through contrasting warm and cool color, as well as through value contrast. The framework for this exercise in functional color is a collection of six or seven gabled houses. Diagram IX-a (which is only *one* possibility) shows an arrangement in which one structure is nearest, the others appearing to recede. Note that the houses are slightly tipped so that opposing axes may create some tension and thus add to the spatial illusion. As usual, a turpentine stain without white is recommended as a beginning.

In developing the composition with white added to the pigment, care should be taken to avoid covering some of the luminous stained areas. Further variation of surface may be had by using the painting knife for some passages. Begin by painting the vertical plane of a building in the

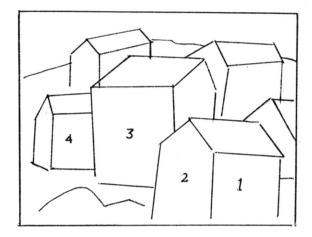

Diagram IX-a

middle space (as in plane No. 3 in the diagram). If this plane is cool and dark, paint No. 2 warm and light. Make No. 1 a lighter variation of No. 3. Number 4 may be warm and dark, etc. Keep the rooftops relatively light and neutral in color. No vertical planes in far buildings should be weaker in color than near planes. Turned upside down the canvas should have an over-all pattern of equal strength in every area. (We cannot repeat too frequently that the preservation of the picture plane is essential to every good composition.) Make the sky a definite gray tone so that a light cloud shape or Ultramarine note in the gray area may carry out the rhythm. By revising the dark pattern throughout for interesting interval the rhythm will be assured.

3. This exercise, related to the foregoing, is based upon an actual set-up and provides greater latitude in shape-making.

Arrange a row of bottles of different sizes, shapes, and colors. (Liqueur and wine bottles, besides being well designed generally, have labels of interesting shape and color.) Place them in such manner that some will appear slightly in front of others. As a preliminary step make a charcoal drawing of the set-up by first covering paper with a uniform dark gray and picking out light pattern with the kneaded eraser. Then strengthen dark shapes. Use just enough line to carry the rhythm throughout the area. Repeat this charcoal exercise several times until you are able to see some planes or tones emerge and others recede, while light and dark shapes create an inventive pattern. The patterns should in no case be the shapes of bottles but may be parts of bottles and whatever labels are visible. In other words, no individual bottle will remain completely defined. This image of a mass of bottles, some in front of others, without the detachment of any one from the rest, is the objective of the drawing (see Fig. 51).

With this preparation begin the painting with stains of color (no drawing), roughly approximating the tonality of the set-up. But do not copy the set-up. Neither should you determine beforehand where each bottle will be; nor should you refer to any of the charcoal studies. In short, improvise the painting. With solid pigment distribute the shapes and colors of labels on top of the stain. When these are placed in a rhythmic pattern, construct parts of bottles in a plausible relationship so that the labels will appear to belong to bottles. Here you will refer to the actual bottle for the plausibility. Paint broadly. Where no specific shapes occur, apply color in simple rectangular passages. Introduce fragments of thin black line for rhythm (possibly abstracted from parts of a bottle, but not for outlining bottles completely or descriptively). This exercise when well done becomes a most satisfactory painting.

4. Paint Exercise 1 in Chapter 5. Use a canvas no smaller than 22" x 28" held vertically. Note that although the drawing is relatively rigid it is possible to attain a free and spirited effect by a bold and relaxed technique. To achieve this the casual brushing in of areas with 1½" house-painter's brushes will be helpful. In addition, some passages may be applied with the painting knife.

Mixing four unusual colors, stain (no white) one color for each plane, then repeat one or two colors in the remaining areas of canvas. When all areas have been stained begin painting with heavy pigment. Distribute geometrical shapes (key shapes, half circles, triangles, etc.,) in black, white, and bright colors. Make the shape on the nearest plane the same color as that in the farthest area. To offset the rigidity of the design, brush with heavy dry pigment across the edges; this will blur them and fuse juxtaposed colors. The effect should be one of different planes telescoped into a unity. The small strong notes will strengthen and integrate the surface. The dual character of the space, recession and flatness, should be the overriding objective.

5. Related to the foregoing, the following exercise is a post-cubist composition employing spatial tensions in an architectonic structure. The composition will consist of large planes of color overlapping each other in such manner as to present simultaneously a flat surface pattern and spatial differentiation.

Six or seven space planes are sufficient for this exercise. The manner

Figure 51

Morris Davidson, *Charcoal Drawing of Bottles*

of stating them will be made clear by preliminary work with construction paper. Since the resulting collage will be quite large (24″ x 30″), the usual packaged construction paper will have to be supplemented by a few larger sheets. Procedure is as follows: Select a large sheet of a pastel color, tear off part of one edge and paste it horizontally on a dark neutral ground so that this ground forms an irregular margin. On one side, from above center, place a vertical plane of prismatic color, top edge torn. Now make a separate unit independent of this. It will be a horizontal unit of three planes of color, one on top of the other, each slightly tipped away from the next. Place this unit on the pastel colored sheet, on the opposite side from the bright vertical plane but lower. Between the two units insert a freely torn shape of a pastel tone lighter than the base sheet but closely related in hue. Diagram IX-b shows such an arrangement.

Note that no suggestion has been made as to the choice of colors or tones for the horizontal unit. The value of the exercise lies in this choice. The objective is to make an arrangement that is harmonious and integrated as well as spatial.

Having made such a collage, one will profit by making a small copy of it in oil. An understanding of the objectives will come from this experience. While these objectives may be clearly pointed out by verbal description and analysis, such demonstration does not in itself prepare one for the making of an effective synthesis. The eminent French painter Villon

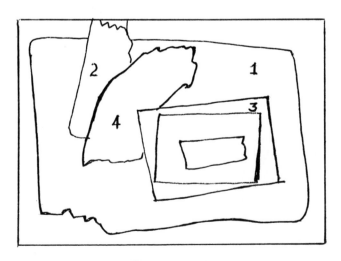

Diagram IX-b

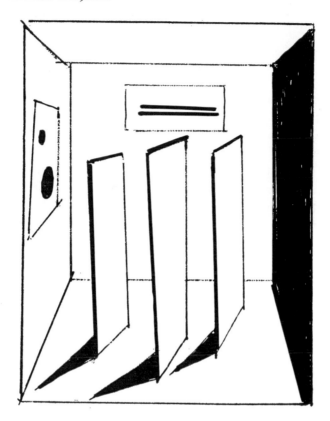

Diagram IX-c

has devoted many years to the invention of color relationships expressing spatial tension in the manner outlined. One's resources as a colorist are most severely tested by this apparently simple problem.

6. The framework is the interior of a room or box as in Exercise 2, Chapter 5. A relatively square canvas, say 20″ x 22″, is best suited. Instead of the table in the foreground, erect vertically three screens reaching to the ceiling but turned in such manner as to thrust into the space, that is, toward the rear wall (see Diagram IX-c). Paint each area in color vivid enough to be harmonious with the black wall, but not harsh or commonplace. Paint patterns of shadow cast on the floor by the screens. Then with clean black line stress some of the vertical edges and one or two diagonals, enough to make the surface design apparent. The linear rhythm will tend to fuse the different planes, relating them to the surface and so providing a unified whole.

PROJECTS IN EVOKING IMAGES THROUGH
ABSTRACT ORGANIZATION

Here we introduce a new procedure, a method used by many abstract painters. This method is in essence a search for plastic meaning. Nothing is visualized beforehand. It is truly described by the phrase "painting for one's amazement."

7. The procedure is to cover a canvas at least 20″ x 24″ with a dozen or more blocks of color *in a stain*. The color should be varied in value, not too prismatic, always transparent. Distribute a few darker tones for balance. Begin painting on top of this stain. Apply heavy passages of color, not completely covering the stained areas. At first these passages will be similar in tone to stains, but as the painting develops new notes of more vivid color will be introduced and distributed. If paint is applied with the knife in free rectangular blocks, vertical and horizontal, some will appear to move forward, others to recede. If a passage of color seems to stand forward, change the shape of a neighboring one by extending a part of it so that it appears to fall behind the salient color. Diagrams IX-d and IX-d′

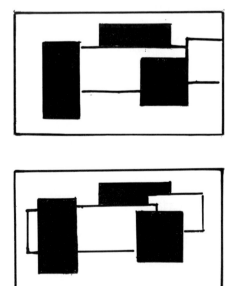

Diagram IX-d Diagram IX-d′

explain this. Continue making extensions until a collection of planes in varying spatial position occurs. To convert these planes to a scene of a complex of buildings it is only necessary to introduce an occasional horizontal plane to represent a roof or a narrow vertical plane to indicate the side of a building.

This exercise is of course an experience in synthetic abstraction. It shifts the painter's mode of thinking from the illustrative impulse to the explorative. It develops a visual imagination which is essential to abstract painting. While the painter working from an explorative concept has no notion of where his painting will lead him, his esthetic sense will automatically determine his choice of colors and their relationship. A painting well done requires no illusions of subject matter to support it. However, the conversion of such an abstract organization into a theme of buildings is of special value to the novice in abstraction in that the experience will change his habitual way of seeing, his customary image. In any case he should make sure that the organization is the best he can achieve. Then the less alteration of the original in the process of conversion the more vital the work is apt to be.

Note: It is not necessary to describe or explain each item; in fact, such meticulous explanation will destroy the rhythmic unity as well as the mystery of the work.

8. This exercise is similar to the one above except that it involves the making of inventive and fanciful shapes rather than simple rectangular blocks and requires greater finesse. It is an imaginary still life.

Stain the canvas with several colors and turpentine to achieve a simple balance of light and dark tones. With a paint rag eliminate sharp edges; the colors should appear to flow into one another. When all areas of canvas are covered begin painting with solid pigment. With a painting knife apply large masses of color in varied shapes without covering all of the stain. These masses need not correspond to tones of stain; on the contrary, the play of varied tones will produce unexpected effects. It is important that the shapes be free of any image or association and that they move in specific directions, that is, that they combine to make an interesting movement over the surface. Turn the canvas upside down and study it. Some of the shapes of color will appear nearer than others. Try mentally to situate each shape with relation to neighboring shapes. See if any accidental illusion of a still life object is possible. If not, turn the canvas until one appears. Strengthen the suggestion with bits of line drawing, sparingly. Find other such illusions but make sure each is on a different spatial level.

Three or four objects are enough. This will insure sufficient surrounding space. In no case should objects be completely outlined. Modify color (or shapes) throughout so that spatial differences will be clear.

Contrast in value makes spatial differences apparent. A light plane between two dark planes will separate the darks most effectively. If the two dark planes are opposed slightly in their axes, that is, one tipped away from the other, the space between will be felt even more. The pulling apart of planes creates tension.

A second version of this imaginative still life is like the first except for the added elements that follow and the general refinement of color. The stain itself should be in low-keyed unusual color, much modified (rather neutral). Restrict heavy passages of color (white added) to four hues, different from the stain but also of mixed, unusual color, not bright. When the illusion of objects is evolved, introduce three or four small vivid notes of color, making at least one note as brilliant in the background as in the foreground. *Do not outline objects.* Spatial differences will be enhanced by stressing luminosity and density of tone, by contrasting values, by overlapping of planes of color, by creating tension through opposing diagonal axes of planes. The small brilliant notes (related to colors previously used) will, if well distributed, hold the painting on the picture plane.

This exercise challenges one's ingenuity and resourcefulness. It combines many elements of painting, the most important of course being the space-relation. See the painting, *Still Life with Fish*, Fig. 52.

PROJECTS IN FLUID SPACE

9. We come now to the first exercise in fluid space. Its primary purpose is to provide the experience of placing masses of color within a given area without tying these masses to the edges of the area. Instead of dividing the total surface into pattern, the object is *to distribute* color passages. When we speak of tying patterns of color to the margins or edges we immediately call to mind a painting by Mondrian; and when we speak of distributing color passages we think of Kandinsky's floating shapes. In distributing these passages we must have in mind (1) that they are to be freely painted, very rapidly and *unfinished*; (2) that the choice of color within the limitation given must be fresh and arresting; (3) that there be a proper balance; (4) that there be variety of size and spacing.

The procedure is as follows: Stain the canvas with a light neutral tone, warm or cool. Mix four hues. (The painting will be limited to these four

Figure 52

Morris Davidson, *Still Life with Fish*

hues but variations may be made by the addition of any other colors provided the latter do not actually destroy the original hue.) Beginning to the right or left of center, using a spatula or a long knife, place a large upright, but slightly tipped, block or passage of color. This should be thickly and boldly applied. The edges should be left as they occur, however ragged or uneven. Slightly above and *behind* this passage place a somewhat smaller darker passage, slightly tipped in the opposite direction to first passage. Then distribute six or seven blocks of various sizes and proportions, all slightly off the vertical and horizontal and all with undefined edges. Make some blocks luminous and others dense. This can be done by using different pigments to make the same hue, and by varying the application of the pigment. See that weight of color provides balance no matter which way the canvas is turned. Note the space-relation suggested by opposing axes of the first two blocks. When balance is established check the study for range of values; if values of blocks are too similar the composition will lack vitality. When the design is established the stain of the background is repainted, varying the surface texturally (with a broad brush) and modifying the values without losing original color. Finally add one small vivid note which will be complementary in color to the general tonality of the painting. For example, if the painting is predominantly yellow-brown, a note of Cerulean Blue, properly placed, will enhance its vitality.

Here it is pertinent to add a technical note. Where a luminous area or note is desired it is well to underpaint. If the note is to be warm, a yellow mixed with quick drying white will provide a base. Over this base, when dry, the final note may be passed with knife or brush. But in either case the stroke must be light and deft in order to be transparent. If the final note is to be a cold one, the underpainting will simply be white, or white diluted to a greenish or violet tint.

This exercise is, as was stated, an introduction to a mode of painting. In itself it is not a formula for a painting, but only the means to an experience with painting ideas and methods now current.

10. The experience of working within the close limitations of the color exercise in yellow in the previous chapter will prepare one for this exercise, a composition in which the use of light and dark interval is explored. Here the range of color will also be limited. With the exception of the light and dark shapes the gamut will be from light yellow to the umbers. (Raw Sienna may be mixed with the yellow.)

Stain the canvas with a few areas, some of Cadmium Yellow Medium, others of Raw Umber. The stain should be kept light. With a spatula or wide brush distribute a few areas of solid Cadmium Yellow. Then place four or five patterns (made with smaller brushes) of Burnt Umber, keeping in mind the need for variety of interval and for balance. Not only in shape and size must the pattern be varied, but also in direction, the tilt or axis. The variation in slant will enhance the rhythm. At this point several areas of the stain should be covered with shapes of grayed white in free, indeterminate blobs. Then on top of these grayed white areas paint five or six precise, inventive shapes of pure white, varying size and axes as in the darks. Repaint the yellow passages in a variety of tones, mixing Cadmium, Sienna, and white, but leaving a few pure yellow notes for accent. No example or diagram is provided here as a guide, because this exercise, while very freely expressed technically, depends almost entirely upon the positions of dark and white symbols. An example or diagram might be followed too closely, or might inhibit one's own sensibility. It is by changing and shifting the symbols or shapes that a rhythmic interval is finally attained. The experience here is everything; the painter must rely upon his own feeling for rhythm.

11. Since so much attention was given in the preceding chapter to the importance of rhythmic line and line fragments in contemporary painting, an exercise in this element is in order. The objective here is to make an over-all pattern of varied line, yet so controlled as to appear a unified entity and not a textile pattern that could be cut off by the yard. The means of establishing this unity are two: the nature of the background and the placing of emphasis in the line itself. These will be discussed in order.

The canvas should be held vertical and not exceed 20″ x 30″. Nuances of near-white are painted over the surface. The white used should be the usual Titanium, not quick-drying. The subtle warm and cool differences should be somewhat varied in value as well, so that some parts will appear darker than others. Within this background place a few delicate notes of color, establishing one such note away from the center as dominant. The appearance of the canvas at this point, while high-pitched and delicate, should be that of a unified surface, the intervals of color and the darker tones creating a balance.

The line is now introduced into the wet paint. It is made by several means: a long No. 2 bristle brush, a small watercolor brush, and the edge of the painting knife. The quality of the line will vary from rigid control (knife) to fluidity (watercolor brush) to ragged brusqueness (bristle brush); from a thin wire-like character to jagged symbols. The weight of the line will control the rhythm so that interest is kept within the canvas in an elliptical movement or orbit. Designed in such manner the canvas will not appear to be a section or fragment of fabric.

As a final step, correct or add to the placing of the color accents in the white ground, or intensify one or two notes. Figure 53 (frontispiece) is a painting based upon the foregoing procedure.

12. A great deal has been said and written about the element of accident in painting. There is no doubt that accident plays an important part even in carefully controlled painting. The element of surprise, of the irrational, is not only exciting because of the novelty and freshness of shape and symbol but because it stimulates our imagination to speculate upon possibilities outside of our experience. But to depend upon accident, to seek deliberately to produce it by various devices results usually in mere formlessness. It catches and titillates the eye for a moment like the iridescence of spilled gasoline on asphalt. What makes accident truly arresting is the incorporation of it into a conscious form. For this reason the emphasis throughout has been placed upon the painter's principles, procedures, and development of sensibility. With the proper background the painter is equipped to make proper use of accident.

All this is preliminary to an exercise in which accident plays an important role.

Make a free composition, that is, a painting in which the tones are not rigidly separated, and in which the brush or knife is used with some abandon. Use many black passages over the painting, varying their size and character. These black symbols or motifs should be consciously placed for rhythm. Put the canvas aside to dry. When the canvas is sufficiently dry to permit overpainting without picking up the original color the second step begins. This is to blot out with heavy impasto white, tinted warm and cool, most of the areas of the background. The black shapes and symbols which create the rhythm will be retained, as will some of the original tones under them. Add a few line fragments or small notes of brilliant color to enhance the rhythm and vitality of the work. Figure 54 is a reproduction of such a work.

A variation of this exercise is one in which a composition of figures, sketchily painted, is the basis. Most of the figures become abstract symbols of figures by the process of blotting out parts with white and adding specific shapes and line pattern. Figure 55 is a painting so produced.

The method of painting here described not only develops the imagination of the student but produces the most surprising results—results impossible to previse. Among contemporary artists who occasionally employ

Figure 54

Morris Davidson, *Dark Intervals on White Ground*

Figure 55

Morris Davidson, *Figure Abstraction*

this means of achieving the unexpected is the celebrated German painter, Fritz Winter (whose painting *Earthbound* is reproduced on page 91). Winter has had entire exhibitions of this style. Even the most imaginative and capable artists discover the advantages of producing the unexpected— provided the accidental effect is made part of a rhythmic unity.

Note that the space in the first version of the exercise is fluid, while that in the figure abstraction is architectonic.

Figure 58

Morris Davidson, *Counterpoint*

A Note on Watercolor for the Painter in Oils

10   Technical information and matters relating to performance are the meat of most manuals on watercolor painting. There is a firmly established tradition in our country that places skill in execution above every other esthetic virtue in this particular branch of art. The best (and most expensive) equipment is recommended to the student and the proper use of it is minutely detailed. Strokes and style are considered as important in watercolor as in golf and tennis. Perhaps this is the reason that large group exhibitions of watercolor reflect a paucity of plastic ideas; there is little imaginative venturing away from stock themes and clichés. One is struck by the great amount of skill and the expert manner in which so little is said.

This situation persists because of the antiquated convention of making watercolor painting a separate activity for specialists—persons whose experience has been more in the realm of craft than in creative art. The practitioner of this speciality refers to himself as a watercolorist rather than as an artist, conscious of the disparity of aims and procedures that exists between him and the painter in oils. Until recently the latter has been quite content to leave the field clear for the specialist, not sharing his interest in the proper way of "laying in a wash."

On the European continent a very different attitude exists. A painter in oils will often exhibit a group of his watercolors in conjunction with his more important works in one-man shows. The European artist considers the medium a means for playful exploration, for surprises, or to make notations for future work. Sometimes he will resort to watercolor to essay slighter or more spontaneous versions of the uniquely personal form that identifies his oils. Sometimes he will turn to his watercolor box for relaxation or play.

A few examples of celebrated oil painters whose watercolors are prized the world over will give point to this European attitude. One thinks first of Cézanne, whose watercolors, although devoid of conventional dash and drama, are yet great. So, too, are those of Paul Klee. Leger, Gromaire, and Dufy are three painters whose world reputations were made in oil painting yet whose watercolors are equally prized. The qualities that impart significance to their work are other than their technical virtues. They are the same qualities that are present in every medium they touch. These artists are mentioned not because they are unique in their mastery of both oil and watercolor, but, on the contrary, because they are typical of thousands of other Continental painters—only they are better known. For these thousands the art of watercolor presents no problems of meeting conventional standards of performance. Each makes his own standards.

Our reason for this brief discourse is that painters accustomed to handling oil are often hesitant to venture into a field noted for its rigid technical demands. It is our belief that much more exciting watercolor than the brand generally esteemed by specialists who serve on art juries would come into being if capable, well trained painters in oil were to include watercolors in their one-man shows. For themselves, their development as artists, and their pleasure in adventuring into a field full of surprises, the experience would be well worthwhile.

It is hardly necessary to say that the painter in oils must explore the characteristics of the watercolor medium and adapt his means of expression to its requirements. The requisite quality, whatever the style, is lightness and clarity; the tones must be transparent, the execution spontaneous and unlabored. The painter accustomed to reworking and overpainting, to density of pigment as a virtue in some instances, will have difficulty at first

Figure 56

Raoul Dufy, *Taormina*. The Collection of S. and I. Ullmann, New York

in acquiring a light touch and clear passage of color. For this reason some suggestions are offered and certain procedures recommended.

Watercolor may be "dry" or "wet." Dry watercolor of course is not dry, it is the application of the wash or stroke to dry paper. Wet watercolor is tone applied to paper previously sponged or dipped. For the beginner exploring the nature of the medium, the dry technique is preferable. A large brush (no. 12) of good quality is an excellent investment. Heavy rough watercolor paper of best quality is, paradoxically, necessary for the beginner but not for the experienced painter. This is because the experienced painter will develop a style suited to a surface of his choice while the beginner will have no notion of the color's potential until he sees it at its best. In any case the cost of the best paper, high as it is, will not be prohibitive, since the first ventures will be kept very small.

A first procedure is to put down a few clear passages of alternately warm and cool color, leaving very fine white spaces between them. The stroke should be rapid and not gone over. The rough paper will impart a sparkle to each area by its own glaze and by leaving minute "pinholes" showing through the color. A rewarding project is the making of such color-note "abstractions" about 4" x 5", varying the tonality (the dominant hue) of each. After such improvisation a more conscious design may be attempted. In this the tones will be restricted to various warm and cool washes of *gray*, leaving white spaces between them. In some of these spaces clear brilliant notes may be circulated to attain both vitality and rhythm. In all these practice color notes the important thing to remember is not to go over a stroke once it is made.

The patterns so made will result in a flat design. Now the learning process becomes the reverse from that of oil painting; it proceeds from the abstract to the representational. This is because competence in making clear, swift statement must be acquired before content is attempted. Having made designs of colors (in some balanced and rhythmic order), the student may turn his attention to illusions of space. A simple exercise for exploring spatial possibilities is to improvise a cluster of houses, one behind another. The procedure will be to juxtapose notes of opposing (warm and cool) color where planes of houses meet, causing these planes to emerge or recede. The effect should be obtained without filling in all areas as in an oil painting. Contrasts of tone will be restricted to the juncture of planes, leaving considerable white paper.

When some confidence in handling the medium is acquired larger compositions may be attempted. The method recommended is to make a pre-

Figure 57

Marcel Gromaire, *The Forest and the Sea*. The Collection of S. and I. Ullmann, New York

157

liminary drawing in pencil on a separate pad. This drawing is for the purpose of clarifying one's ideas but it should not be copied onto the watercolor paper. Painting within pencil lines results in a dry, pedestrian performance. Further, the water-colorist should be free to change or improvise as he proceeds. The manner of interpreting the sketch is important. In general, it is well to establish a few wet areas on the paper even when the major part is to be dry. These may be subtle or delicate in tone, just deep enough to suppress the whiteness of the paper. In a representational work the actual painting is best begun in the middle area so that one may create illusions of space behind and space in front.

As stated earlier the experience in working on dry paper is only a prelude to the search for a more personal expression. The sponged or wetted paper will more likely provide the springboard for the imagination. It is less direct but more evocative. The technique in working wet depends only upon one's inventiveness. For the beginner, however, a few hints may be in order. The paper is placed on a board, its edges securely fastened by masking tape or gummed paper. It is then lightly sponged. The color is brushed, sometimes dropped onto the moist surface so that it will diffuse in gentle gradations. When the surface is half dry, stronger notes of color may be distributed. A sharpened stick with India ink may be drawn into the watercolor; colored inks may be used, the flexible stopper serving as a drawing instrument. Of late the Japanese brush has become popular for calligraphic effects and the Japanese ink-stick has given an entirely new look to present-day watercolor. Its charcoal tones richly set off the glowing washes. Sometimes touching up the wet watercolor with bright opaque tones like Naples Yellow, the Cadmiums, and Chinese White will give an added vitality to the work.

Mixed techniques will not possess the sparkle of pure watercolor but other desirable ends may be achieved by them. Casein pigment, which dries opaque, may create a spatial play with transparent washes, and chalks or crayon will produce unusual effects in combination with broad washes.

Considerations of an esthetic nature should determine the choice of technique. Imagery as well as washes should be fresh. In saying this we are only repeating that a fine watercolor is a work of the imagination, not just a craft. There are clichés in color as well as in theme, and both are to be shunned. Above all a watercolor should be rhythmical. There must exist an interplay of movement, whether of line, or color note, or dark, any or all of which may make a felt unity.

We reproduce a few examples of contemporary watercolor which ex-

Figure 59

Morris Davidson, *Blue Ambiance*

press the concepts and forms of the painter in oils while retaining the qualities of the more spontaneous medium. The painting *Taormina* (Fig. 56) by Raoul Dufy is a playful, imaginative "short-hand" description, the artist's impression of the Silician town seen from below. The volumes of trees, walls, and buildings are converted into motifs or symbols in Chinese fashion. These motifs make up the spirited rhythm of the composition by the manner of their distribution. Freshness and spontaneity of statement impart a spirit—a pleasurable response to the scene—that is contagious.

Very different is the watercolor of Marcel Gromaire, *Forest and Sea* (Fig. 57). Profusion of ink line over sombre tones precludes a feeling of spontaneity. But in its place there is the glow of color and light behind the darker shapes. While these dark shapes are distributed in an abstract pattern, they are used in some instances to express volume, as in the rocks, tree trunks, etc. The style appears to be more abstract than the Dufy yet the retention of volume in reality links the total composition to cubist representation. In any case it is the counterpart of the painter's oils; it expresses his personal concept and form without concession to conventional watercolor technique.

The two watercolors of the author, *Counterpoint* (Fig. 58) and *Blue Ambiance* (Fig. 59), are examples of non-figurative watercolors in current idioms. Figure 58 is in a geometrical style in which dynamic movement is expressed not only by the line pattern but by opposing axes of the triangles, the spatial tension between the two notes of deep yellow and the intervals of the dark rectangles. Spontaneity of statement is visible in the variation of line pressure and the hasty calligraphy. The space is fluid but there are suggestions of overlapping planes. This, together with the geometrical character of the composition, reveals a background of Cubism.

Figure 59 is structurally very unlike the other. It is entirely fluid and quite placid. There are no defined patterns, not even symbols or shapes. The relaxed calligraphy, done in ink on a wet surface, plays over the modulated blue background to create a rhythm. The rhythm is enhanced by the distribution of small notes of yellow. The style of this watercolor, like its spatial concept, derives from Chinese painting.

The painter in oils who turns to watercolor periodically for the reasons stated earlier should bear in mind that the medium affords the most intimate and spontaneous expression of his total being, his "gestalt"; it is the handwriting of his stored-up consciousness. He should not permit conventions of craft to inhibit him.

A Note
in Conclusion

11 There is an old saying, "A method is known by its results as a tree is known by its fruit." The exercises and painting projects of the preceding pages have been executed by scores of students, a good percentage of whom are now exhibiting painters. Merely to go through the discipline of working out problems, however, as one might dutifully attack homework, will yield little. The essential factors in deriving the most benefit from the work are two: (1) a desire for, if not a delight in, difficult exploration; (2) a sensuous feeling for pigment.

Regarding the first requisite it may be worthwhile to recount an incident.

A European painter of note, whose command of English was not too good, was asked to give a talk on contemporary painting. He succeeded in communicating to his audience his very original ideas by dint of expressive gesture and quaint but pithy locutions. At the end he was asked by a listener if he would care to define art. "Only for myself," he said. "Art is like this." And he began rising on his toes and extending his arms upward until he could go no further. "You see," he said, "for me it is effort beyond possible."

This straining to exceed one's known potential is for some a painful undertaking. For others it is a most exciting challenge. It is a matter of one's make-up—one's temperament and sense of adventure. Some enjoy exploration even when it appears fruitless; others suffer frustration for want of a prevision of their effort. A student of this latter category will sometimes ask of a painter, "At what point does suffering end and satisfaction in painting begin?" Painting is like wrestling. The tremendous effort put forth by a wrestler can be most enjoyable—when he knows the holds, when he is experienced and resourceful. The student who has explored the principles of painting does not shrink from extending himself beyond the possible. In fact such intense effort may be a source of deep enjoyment because it reveals to the painter capacities beyond his awareness.

As for the sensuous feeling for pigment, this is innate and unteachable. Its presence or its absence is revealed in every work. The element of performance is dependent upon it. For this very reason it is impossible to regard the material of this book as a course, like English 5 or History 2A, or any other subject where application and intelligence alone determine accomplishment.

Yet without objectives, without a clear understanding of purpose, painting is only a pastime; one may revel in pigment and joyfully paint hours on end as sport, as therapy, or for cultural "growth." To paint with purpose is to project all of one's resources, one's sensibilities, feelings, and concept of organization onto the canvas. Such total effort is a prerequisite for art.

Index

Index

A

B

165